TESTIMONIALS

"I was desperate to find my partner, and Rachel's coaching helped me realize that I was going about dating the wrong way. With her help, I successfully found my husband within two months of working with her!"

—Megan Banks, Los Angeles, CA

"This book may be aimed at women, but it's a great list of what not to do for guys, too! Rachel lays out her lessons with personal stories that entertain while they advise, and I was truly sad that this book had to end."

—David Gannon, Rockville, MD

"I highly recommend Rachel as a relationship coach. Her calm demeanor and sense of humor make her so much fun to work with. She has a superb understanding of finding your true love, and her experiences/stories have taught me so much. Her advice and lessons are really insightful. And guess what?! Now I'm engaged!"

—Sydney Frankel, Tampa, FL

"This is a book that I will likely re-read and reference multiple times. It's simple and straightforward and gives excellent advice for finding and keeping my perfect mate. I wish I had applied these lessons years ago."

—Danielle Morgan, Portland, OR

"Rachel is the best! She has a pleasant and friendly disposition, and I feel completely comfortable talking to her about my dating catastrophes. Because of her help, I have a clear understanding of what I need to do to find my perfect man. No more catastrophes for me!"

—Heather Johnson, Chicago, IL

"I love how this book starts out each chapter with a lesson and then goes into the author's personal stories. Some stories are hilarious, while others are touching and sad. Rachel's writing resonated with me, and I'm comforted to know that we have all faced the same dating challenges."

—Elizabeth Parks, New York, NY

"Rachel wrote a relatable book with humorous anecdotes. It was a quick, enjoyable read, and I know that following her lessons will help guide me toward my soulmate. I recommend this book for any woman who wants clear, simple dating advice to find your perfect mate."

—Allison Tillman, Washington, DC

"I adore Rachel's coaching and writing style. She has a plethora of knowledge that she shares with her audience, and I'm drawn to her friendly, welcoming personality. After having a few coaching sessions with her, she gave me the skills and confidence to pursue my perfect woman. Thanks to Rachel, I'll soon be married to the woman of my dreams!"

—Jordan Jacobs, Boston, MA

DATE TO FIND YOUR SOULMATE

How to get the man of your dreams through strategic and successful dating techniques

RACHEL SCHEER

ISBN: 978-1-64184-495-6 (paperback)
ISBN: 978-1-64184-494-9 (hardback)
ISBN: 978-1-64184-496-3 (ebook)

TABLE OF CONTENTS

PART ONE
LOOK OUT FELLAS, HERE I COME!

Breakups, the grieving period, and how to enjoy your single
life before jumping back into the dating scene.
I'll kickbox my way to happiness if that's what it takes.

The ins and outs of online dating, profile pictures, and conversation patterns so you can avoid all the losers and save yourself hours of misery.
I think you've been using the same blurry profile picture for 30 years.

Making assumptions when meeting a potential dating partner, how looks can be deceiving, and the "perfect on paper" myth.
I've always wondered what it would be like to pee on someone.

First date preparation and etiquette so you can master the art of dating and figure out if you're interested in a second date.
The back seat of my mom's car is an ideal make-out spot.

Red flags in dating and relationships so you can stay away from guys that show clear warning signs right from the start.
An erection in the pool is such a turn on.

The trouble with dating guys who are stuck in the closet and haven't figured out their own identities yet.
I feel like the third wheel on my own date.

Different life stages you go through and why age matters when
figuring out who you should spend time dating.
I promise we're not all gold diggers.

PART TWO
FROM DATING TO DEEPER COMMITMENT

How to avoid being stuck in the friend zone so you can dive
into an exclusive relationship when the time is right.
I'll be cursed for a year after no New Year's kiss.

What type of compatibility is needed in a relationship so you
can find and date a guy who fulfills all your desires.
I want you to be my missing puzzle piece.

Guys you shouldn't date, emotional affairs, and ex-wife drama
that will send you running for the hills.
I can't believe I have become "the other woman."

The truth about sexual issues and STDs so you can learn how
to protect yourself and understand why you're not in the
mood for intimacy.
Unfortunately, Viagra doesn't solve all sexual problems.

Changing your personality for a guy and letting him control you so you can keep him interested in the "fake" version of you. *Don't you dare try to put out my fire.*

The lowdown on mental health and addiction so you can avoid dating guys who aren't ready for a committed relationship. *Piña Coladas are magically delicious.*

How your five senses play a part in dating so you can avoid guys who irritate you and stick with men who delight your senses. *If you have the voice of an angel, your looks don't matter.*

PART THREE
CREATING A LIFE TOGETHER

Having cold feet, picture-perfect dates, and how your intuition kicks into gear at the optimal time and shouldn't be ignored. *Chemistry is a tricky thing.*

When moving for a guy is appropriate so you can make smart choices and not end up in a new city alone and single. *I'll drive 3,000 miles during a snowstorm to be with you.*

Waiting for a guy to make a decision about your future so
you can stop putting your life on hold and start making your
dreams come true.
I know I'll get my big break eventually.

Requirements that make or break a relationship so you can
clarify your needs and confirm that you and the guy both
want the same things.
Going to a movie apparently equals cheating.

Behaviors to pay attention to while on vacation and other
places so you can decide if you're willing to tolerate this guy
forever.
There must be a dead body in your suitcase.

Sex mishaps, car accidents, and how you dwell on past mistakes
instead of focusing on your bright future.
Let's take a drive to the emergency room after our date.

FOREWORD

People refer to me as the "Mother of Sex Coaching" because I was the one who created this new profession back in 1993. I was a star on the rise in my field. By 2007, I had already earned a PhD in human sexuality, been President of the American Association of Sexuality Educators, Counselors, and Therapists (AASECT), enjoyed a media presence on television, radio, and print, and written multiple books and articles on human sexuality.

After giving a presentation about my latest book, *The Art of Sex Coaching: Expanding Your Practice*, a young woman named Rachel Scheer walked up to me, eager to learn more. As luck would have it, I was creating an online sex coaching training program. I needed extra support to craft it with the essential information and teaching elements it required, while also making it fun and dynamic.

This young, bright woman volunteered to assist me, and thus began our journey. We spent many late nights pouring all our time and energy into a program that is now successfully offered to hundreds of students worldwide at SexCoachU.com.

This original sex coaching program has earned international acclaim and represents a diversity-focused and humanistic sexological perspective that is unmatched by most comprehensive programs in sexology.

But it's not just about sex!

(Which is what you'll see in the pages of this book.)

I empathize with all the single people in the world. Dating has progressed in the past fifty years, and not necessarily in the best way. There are endless venues and places for singles to meet, especially in the online dating scene, but authentic communication and respectful dating etiquette have practically disappeared.

That's why Rachel is so powerful and skilled.

With her upbeat personality and entertaining dating stories, it was always a pleasure to have her around. She was very sure of herself and knew what she was looking for in a partner, but she continued to have dating disasters that she shared with me.

I patiently listened and coached her through relationship issues when she asked for help. She became a better coach after working through her own barriers and applying that for her clients seeking similar help.

Today, she walks the walk as she guides others.

As Rachel's mentor, I watched her learn and grow so much as a person and as a coach. We shared our independent thoughts about life and love while she attended all my seminars and helped me work out the kinks in my sex coaching training program by completing its first rendition with competency and excellence.

In addition to helping me develop portions of the emerging content, she was the first student to take all the courses available at that time and become the first official graduate. She was on her way to becoming a shining example of positive sexuality and relationship finesse!

I was proud of Rachel's success, and I could tell that she was shaping up to be an exceptional coach. After her two years of training, I urged her to start her own coaching practice. She fervently plowed ahead with her new business and networked all over Los Angeles to get her name out there.

While growing her business, she continued to date and learn new lessons about love, sex, and intimacy along the way. She passed on this knowledge to her coaching clients, which allowed them to adjust their dating methods and find loving partners.

Rachel openly shares her experiences in this book, and her dating lessons are crucial to follow if you want to find lasting love. She has spent twenty-five years of her life dating and knows what she's talking about.

If you're struggling to find a romantic partner, Rachel's lessons will give you the inside story from a woman who has seen, done, and grown from it all!

This book is a delight that will guide you and uplift your spirits with insightful lessons, advice, and tips for finding the love of your life—*and* becoming a better human through it all.

May it bring you great joy and evoke your passion for finding your mate by following the classy expertise of the one and only Rachel Scheer.

With lasting love,
Patti Britton, PhD, Founder of Sex Coach U and
world-recognized Clinical Sexologist

DEDICATION

To all the single women who have unsuccessfully been looking for their life partners for many years. I'm excited for you to find the man of your dreams after following the lessons in this book!

DISCLAIMER

Names and identifying characteristics have been changed to protect the privacy of individuals. The stories in this book are real, with some details altered to tell an abridged version. These stories took place over a twenty-five-year period of my life, and they are not told in chronological order.

YOU'RE IN FOR A TASTY TREAT

Hi! It's Rachel!

Are you single?

Ever wonder if you'll die sad and alone, maybe as a "crazy cat lady"?

I totally get it.

I used to worry about that, too.

And then everything changed.

And now I know exactly what not to do and what types of men to avoid.

But how, you may ask?

Throughout my adult life, I've had a few long-term relationships, some casual flings, and hundreds of first dates. In this book, I am sharing my dating lessons with you that I've learned from twenty-five years of dating.

(And from decades of studying, reading books, taking courses, and gaining knowledge from established coaches and methodologies.)

Every mistake I made brought me one step closer to finding my true love. Hopefully, you'll learn from my mistakes (at least, the ones I've chosen to share) and find a clearer, more direct path to finding your forever mate.

I have coaching certifications in love, sex, singles, and couples, and I'm passionate about coaching others so they find and keep successful relationships.

I enjoy getting to the heart of people's dating and relationship issues so I can guide them along their journey to love.

I've used my experience and education, along with my intuition, to create love connections for clients, friends, and acquaintances.

I have so much practical wisdom to share.

If you follow my lessons, you *will* find the man of your dreams.

If you want the brutal truth, come to me.

If you want to learn how to build a strong foundation and find your soulmate, this book is for you.

Your ideal guy is waiting right around the corner!

Let's get you there, the right way, and right on time.

Here's to the two of you,
Rachel

If you're the type of person who likes to take immediate action to make your dreams come true, then I invite you to schedule a no-hassle "Find Your Soulmate" discovery call today by going to LoveLaughLeisure.com.

HOW TO USE THIS BOOK AND WHAT TO EXPECT

When it comes to dating, I've been there, done that. With hundreds of first dates under my belt, I've had every type of experience imaginable. Some dates were good, others were excellent, and the majority were just plain awful.

In this book, I take you through a journey. You'll learn my dating lessons and some personal stories that relate to each one so you can find your soulmate.

If you skimmed through the table of contents, you may have noticed that there are 20 chapters. Don't worry! I broke it down into three sections.

- Part One: Look out fellas, here I come!
  This is when you start dating and everything is new and thrilling.

- Part Two: From dating to deeper commitment
  A deeper commitment unfolds as you learn more about each other.

- Part Three: Creating a life together
  You move into a life-long partnership with your soulmate.

Some of the wacky, wonderful mishaps that happen at the beginning of dating can suddenly creep up months or years later. Although there are three sections, you will have different experiences with every guy you date. An incident with one guy on a first date could be similar to what you face with another guy after six months of dating.

You can skip around or read straight through, but it's important to understand the main lesson of every chapter. Once you master these dating techniques, you will have the proper skills to find your life partner.

What you'll find in the following pages is absolutely applicable to you, no matter how much dating experience you have. If you've never been on a date before, this book will set you up for success. If you just got out of a serious relationship, you'll learn how to find the right guy this time instead of wasting your time with losers.

You're about to discover essential dating strategies that you can use right away in your love life. These lessons are presented in a clear, simple, and direct way, so you'll have no doubt about how and when to use them.

This isn't like any other book you've read. It's saturated with takeaways. It's based on proven methods that have been used by thousands of people to attract their soulmates.

Although it's nonfiction, I've written this book as a narrative that's conversational and filled with stories, humor, anecdotes, and action steps to help you find the man of your dreams.

HERE'S WHAT TO EXPECT

- Breaking up with a guy may feel like the worst thing ever to happen to you, but it's actually putting you on a better path toward love. The guy you broke up with was obviously wrong for you, and after mourning the end of that relationship, you can focus on yourself and your awesome life as a single woman before jumping back into the dating scene (Chapter 1).

- Once you're ready to find love again, it's time to test online dating. There are lots of freaks and crazies that take over dating apps, but with the right communication methods, you'll get dates with worthy guys in no time (Chapter 2).

- You'll soon realize that guys aren't always what they seem, but taking a chance on someone who isn't your usual type is sometimes the best way to meet your perfect partner (Chapter 3).

- When you schedule a first date with a guy you're excited to meet, there are certain rules you should follow before, during, and after your date to ensure that everything goes smoothly (Chapter 4). Paying attention to red flags is also crucial so you can avoid guys that show clear warning signs right from the start (Chapter 5).

- If the guy hasn't figured out his own identity yet, then you may want to steer clear of him for now (Chapter 6). Knowing what stage of life you're in is important so you don't waste your time with a guy who wants something different at this point in your life. If you're ready to get married, but he still wants to play the field, you'll have to go your separate ways (Chapter 7).

- As you get deeper into dating, you'll start to question whether you're just hookup buddies or moving toward an exclusive relationship. It's a confusing time in dating and can get frustrating not knowing if you're headed toward long-term commitment (Chapter 8).

- What matters more than anything is that you're compatible with the guy you're dating. You want someone who fulfills all your needs, and you'll start to notice if this guy could be your soulmate (Chapter 9). If he's married or still dealing with an ex, you don't want to spend another second on him (Chapter 10).

- Eventually, sex comes into play in the dating process. Maybe it's immediate, or perhaps you've decided to wait. Either way, you should protect yourself and understand what intimacy means to you (Chapter 11). If you find yourself changing your personality to appease the guy, it's time to take a stand and be true to yourself (Chapter 12).

- It's difficult to handle issues with mental health and addiction, so if they become a problem in the relationship, you'll, unfortunately, have to give him time and space to heal or move on to a guy who's more stable (Chapter 13).

- Don't forget how vital your five senses are. Not just in life, but in love as well (Chapter 14). Plus, your sixth sense, intuition, will kick into gear at the optimal time and shouldn't be ignored (Chapter 15).

- If the guy lives far away or has to suddenly move across the country, it's scary to decide if moving with him is appropriate (Chapter 16). But if you keep waiting for him to make a decision about your future, you may put your life on hold and never follow through on your dreams (Chapter 17).

- Making a relationship work takes effort, and an essential part of dating means determining if you both require the same things in life (Chapter 18). As a potential life partner, you'll definitely want to go on vacation together to see how well you interact when you're both in a new environment (Chapter 19).

- Finally, you must accept that mistakes happen. There's no point in dwelling on your past and remembering all the guys you shouldn't have dated. Your love life will continue and progress as it should, so just look forward into your bright future with the man of your dreams (Chapter 20).

HOW FINDING YOUR SOULMATE CAN MAKE THE WORLD A BETTER PLACE

As the world changes, people are partnering up to get through the chaos of life with someone who understands them. We're all searching for love and companionship, and spending a lifetime alone isn't appealing for most.

This book will teach you how to find the love you deserve and stop wasting your time dating losers!

You can make the world a better place by finding your soulmate.

How, you might ask?

Let me tell you a quick story.

I went for a relaxing stroll in my neighborhood recently.

I've taken countless walks around the block in the past, and I've never gotten a second glance from anyone.

There are always people walking by or working on their lawns, but we never say "hi" to each other. These aren't unfriendly people, but we just don't greet strangers in my town.

But this day was different.

As I took my stroll on this breezy day, something unusual happened.

Every single person said "hi" to me.

In fact, people who were deep in conversation intentionally turned toward me and gave me a big smile and warm greeting.

People across the street waved to get my attention just to say "hi."

Drivers stopped in the middle of the road and rolled their windows down to say "hello."

It was incredible. I felt like I was in an alternate reality.

There was one major difference to my stroll.

I wasn't alone this time. I was walking with my soulmate.

Everyone sensed our aura of positivity and happiness, and it rubbed off on them. They wanted a piece of our loving energy, and we willingly gave them a taste by simply saying "hello" and smiling back at them.

We made our neighborhood a better place that day just from walking around the block. We improved the mood of everyone that crossed our path.

You have the power to spread love and joy throughout the world.

Imagine what you can accomplish if you let your loving energy fill the atmosphere with hope and happiness.

Once you find your soulmate, the sky will be brighter. Your neighbors will be happier. And the world will be a better place.

I'M RACHEL;
IT'S NICE TO MEET YOU

How the hell did I get here?

I sometimes wonder that myself...

As a teenager, I was completely boy-crazy. My life revolved around boys. I plastered my walls with posters of cute movie stars and stayed up all night fantasizing about meeting them.

In school, my only motivation to go to class was to see my crush. I had perfect attendance, mainly because I was eager to spend all day staring at the boy I was interested in that year.

I filled diaries with conversations I had with these boys, and I added every detail of my emotions and analysis of our interactions.

I longingly gawked at teenagers in love, and I watched with curiosity as they argued about mundane topics and broke up. As an inquisitive person, I asked questions to learn more about how they fell in love and why they split up.

My childish diary scribbles turned into meaningful dating lessons that I learned from others and my own experiences throughout the years. I discovered that everyone needs help with their romantic relationships, so I took all the knowledge I gained and became a relationship coach.

I made it my mission to help single women find love. I've seen love in its purest form, and it's an absolutely beautiful sight.

I desperately want you to find your soulmate so you can live out your life with the man of your dreams by your side. Now let's get started.

PART ONE

LOOK OUT FELLAS,
HERE I COME!

CHAPTER 1
I HAVE THE BED ALL TO MYSELF!

You just went through another heart-wrenching breakup. You feel lonely and depressed and wonder if you'll ever be happy again. You could hide under the covers forever. Or you could accept that the relationship is over, give yourself time to heal, and make room in your heart for the guy you're meant to be with.

You *will* be joyful and radiant and magnificent again! It may take a few days, a few weeks, or a few months, but you *will* get over this breakup and feel so much better about yourself. When you go through a breakup, you have to deal with a huge loss in your life. You need time to mourn.

THE KUBLER-ROSS MODEL OF THE FIVE STAGES OF GRIEF

1. Denial

2. Anger

3. Bargaining

4. Depression

5. Acceptance

Once you complete these stages and accept your breakup, you'll be able to see how wonderful life can be as a single woman.

MY EXPERIENCE WITH THE STAGES OF GRIEF

I genuinely thought I was going to marry Keith. We dated for over a year, and when he dumped me, it felt like my heart was ripped out of my chest. Without realizing it, I went through the five stages of grief in order.

1. **Denial:** I didn't believe we were broken up at first. It didn't seem real to me. When friends talked about Keith in the past tense, as if he didn't exist anymore, I corrected them by saying he wasn't officially my ex. I denied the fact that we weren't together.

2. **Anger:** I went to kickboxing classes and kicked the crap out of the punching bag. I had so much anger bubbling inside of me, but I couldn't shake the anger I felt toward Keith. I wanted him to suffer for the pain he caused me.

3. **Bargaining:** I took an online course on "how to get your ex back." I called him a few times and tried to bargain with him to take me back. He wasn't interested in rekindling the flame.

4. **Depression:** I fell into a deep depression. I didn't have the energy to do anything. Even food, which normally brings me so much joy, was tasteless to me. I stopped talking to all friends and family and became a hermit.

5. **Acceptance:** Exactly four months after our breakup, I woke up one day and accepted that it was over. My grieving period had ended, and I was ready to face the world again.

In all my breakups, I've gone through the five stages of grief. Not necessarily in order, and some stages lasted much longer than others. With one guy I dated, I went through the stages while we were still together. I knew in my heart that we weren't going to last, so by the time we did break up, I had already accepted it and moved on. The day we broke up, I went to a party. All my friends were amazed that I looked so alive and energetic after ending a two-year relationship. I felt like a newer, better version of myself, and I was grateful to be single.

Reasons Being Single Is the Best

1. You have complete control over everything. You get to do whatever you want and go wherever you want.

2. You have the bed all to yourself. You can sprawl out and have a peaceful night's sleep without being woken up by snoring. You can sleep all weekend if you want to.

3. You don't have to compromise on a movie or TV show to watch. You get to watch whatever you please.

4. You can order food from all your favorite restaurants and eat everything yourself. You don't have to split the last eggroll.

5. You can plan a girls' night out without checking with anyone or needing to get permission.

6. You get to focus on yourself. If you've wanted to take a class or learn a new skill, now is your chance.

7. You can have the life you've always imagined. Want to have a relaxing day at the spa? Go for it! You deserve it.

8. You get to explore your passions and hobbies without worrying about making time for a partner.

9. You can figure out who you are. You are a unique individual with impressive qualities.

10. You can spend more time with family and friends. Your loved ones will always be there for you, so make the most of your time with them.

Over 45% of adults are single. Wouldn't you rather be single and free than be stuck in a dead-end relationship? You may be jealous of your married friends, but they are most likely envious of your life. You have no one weighing you down or preventing you from following your dreams.

If you do want to get married, you're in a much better position than your unhappily married friends. Once you get through mourning your last breakup, you can follow my dating lessons and find the man of your dreams.

SUMMARY

Breakups suck, but once you complete the five stages of grief, you'll be free to enjoy your life as a sexy, sophisticated, single woman!

CHAPTER 2
DATING APP OVERLOAD

If I could get an award for going on the most online dates, I think I'd win. I've chatted with thousands of guys online, met hundreds of them, and the numbers take a nosedive after that. Few first dates have turned into second ones. I also would have saved myself a lot of time and effort if I did a better job of weeding out the freaks.

ATROCIOUS DATING PROFILE PICTURES

1. Shirtless/practically naked: I get that you're proud of your body, but put a frickin' shirt on!

2. Working out: Again, I can tell you want to show off your muscles, but I don't need to see you doing bicep curls.

3. Holding a fish: I thought this was just a regional thing, but apparently, guys all over the world love to show off that they caught a fish. That just doesn't appeal to me.

4. Holding a baby: Is it your baby? A friend's? Did you steal it? It's unclear, and it doesn't make me believe you love babies.

5. Groups: Which one are you? I don't want to strain my eyes to figure out which person is the common denominator in five group shots.

6. Blurry: Are you afraid to show yourself? Then I guess I'm afraid to meet you.

7. Animals: Maybe you have a cute dog, but I want to see what *you* look like, not your pet.

8. Not current: It looks like you wore that outfit in the '90s. Do you have any current pics to show me? Possibly something from the past year (not decade).

9. Creepy: You look like an ax murderer. Why is there blood on your clothes?

10. Unsmiling: One serious picture is acceptable, I suppose, but I'd rather see you smiling and having fun. No mugshots, please.

11. No full body: If you have six pictures, but they're all up close and only show your face, it makes me wonder what's going on down there.

12. No face: I've also seen the opposite, where you only show your body and no face pictures. What are you hiding?

13. Nature: I can find a nature photo on the internet. Why is this picture on your profile if you're not even in it?

14. Hat and sunglasses: If you have a hat on in every picture, I assume you're bald. The sunglasses don't make you any cooler. Don't be afraid to show off your beautiful, bald head.

15. Multiples: If you take ten pictures of yourself wearing the same outfit from different angles, they're basically the same picture. Get some variety.

16. Far away: Your photos have a lovely background, but it looks like you're hundreds of miles away. Sorry, I don't have X-ray vision.

17. Filters: Are you ten years old? Feel free to send your friend a picture of you looking like a cat, but it's not appropriate for a dating profile.

18. With a date: You have your arm around a stunning woman, and I don't think she's your sister. Is she currently your girlfriend? Should I be jealous?

There are many other awful types of profile pictures I've seen, but these are the first that come to mind. The list applies to both men and women. If you have doubts about your pictures, ask a few people for advice. Having a variety of photos that show off who you are is the best plan. And I won't tell you to swipe left every time you see one of the above types of pictures because there will be no one left to match with.

Now let's say you do match with someone and start sending each other messages. Normal communication rarely exists in the online dating world. I've mainly received ridiculous messages that make me question the sanity of men who use dating apps.

COMMON PATTERNS I'VE SEEN IN CONVERSATION

1. He says "hi" and then disappears.

2. You engage in meaningful conversation for a few days, and then he disappears.

3. You engage in meaningful conversation for a few days, and then he suddenly gets oddly perverted.

4. He tells you that he's not looking for anything serious. He just wants to have some fun. (I appreciate the honesty, at least.)

5. He reveals deep, personal stuff, and when you reciprocate, he gets uncomfortable and ignores you.

6. He blocks you out of the blue.

7. He says, "wanna fuck?" as an opening line.

8. He sends a dick pic.

9. He asks you out and then never confirms plans.

10. He asks you out, schedules a date, and then doesn't show up.

11. He writes a long-winded reply to your question, and when you send a follow-up message, he freaks out about revealing too much.

12. He sends a few messages in a row, and if you don't reply within thirty seconds, he calls you a bitch for ignoring him.

Since my coaching clients continue having all these online dating mishaps, you might wonder why I urge them to keep trying. Well, 39% of couples meet online these days, while fewer and fewer meet through friends, family, or work. There are tons of websites and apps to communicate with prospects and get dates, and there are hopefully at least a few normal men left. I have plenty of clients who met their partners through an online venue, so I know it's possible!

Some of my friends just want to have sex, and online dating is a nifty way to find a one-night stand. If you're visiting a different city for the weekend, you can just swipe right on a few people and get a date within minutes. It's much more challenging to find a guy interested in a committed relationship, which is the online dating goal of my clients.

Some sites recommend a detailed profile, and those are the ones that are more beneficial to their users. Unfortunately, with today's swiping mentality, people easily dismiss potential partners based only on a picture and don't read a word of the profile. Oh, another guy holding a fish? Swipe left!

Lots of people continuously swipe left, knowing there are millions of options out there. Or they swipe right on everyone and meet as many people as possible. However, they don't give anyone a real chance and swipe right on a few hundred other guys while they're on a date.

If you give everyone a chance, tell them what you're looking for, and have a phone conversation before meeting in person, it will save you a lot of time and heartache. The phone conversation is equal to meeting them at a party and having a quick chat before exchanging numbers. You might realize you don't click while talking, and so you feel that a date in person is unnecessary. That just saved you a few hours of pain.

In this phone call, you should also clarify what your reason is for dating. If you're looking for a commitment, while the other person just wants to play the field, you can decide if meeting in person makes sense.

There's always the chance that you have a fabulous phone conversation, but then you don't feel any attraction or chemistry in person. That's why you shouldn't have lots of lengthy phone calls and delay meeting in person.

If you live far apart, virtual dates are the way to go. You can get to know each other on a deeper level from the beginning. Unfortunately, you run the risk of feeling a strong emotional connection without having chemistry.

Online dating can take many directions.

WHEN YOUR ONLINE DATING ADVENTURES DON'T END WELL

1. You meet immediately and feel nothing.

2. You text and talk for weeks, and then meet and feel nothing.

3. You meet immediately and jump into bed because you have chemistry. Then you get to know each other and realize there's no long-term potential.

4. You text and talk for weeks. Because you feel a tiny bit of attraction, you force a relationship. You've already dedicated so much time and energy into this person that you want to make it work, but it falls apart soon after.

Despite all the losers you keep meeting, you continue to try online dating, hoping it'll lead to true love.

WHEN YOUR ONLINE DATING ADVENTURES DO END WELL

1. You meet after a few texting exchanges and a ten-minute phone call, feel sparks, and start dating the man of your dreams. You fall in love, get married, and live happily ever after.

2. You meet immediately and jump into bed because you have chemistry. You like him a lot and worry that you ruined your chances by having sex too soon. Luckily, he feels the same way and calls you for a second date. You continue dating, fall in love, get married, and live happily ever after.

3. You talk virtually for weeks or even months. You develop a strong emotional connection but wonder if there's any chemistry. You finally meet in person, fall in love, get married, and live happily ever after.

You'll never know if online dating will work for you unless you give it a try. There are plenty of different options, and you can join multiple sites and apps or just stick with one. I found that the best method for online dating is to have a few texting exchanges within a few days. Then have one or two phone conversations or virtual chats (no more than an hour long). If you still like him, then try to meet in person as soon as possible. You may feel a connection, and you may not. That's life.

ONLINE DATING MISTAKES I'VE MADE

1. There was only one blurry picture on his profile. When I asked for another photo, he said he'd send me one later. He wanted to talk on the phone, so we talked for hours and hours. He called me every night for two weeks, and I felt so connected to him from our long, deep conversations. He kept changing the subject when I asked about seeing another photo, but I hoped and prayed that he was as attractive as I imagined. Of course, he wasn't. We met, and I was disgusted by his looks.

   Lesson: Get clear pictures of him before meeting.

2. I agreed to drive extremely far to meet him because his car wasn't working, and he had to be dropped off by a friend. We had a decent first date, and then we planned a second date for the following weekend in a more centralized location. He called me the day before our second date to ask if I'd drive to him

again. It was a five-hour round-trip journey, but I liked him and agreed. After two hours on the road, I got a message from him that he had to cancel. I never heard from him again after that.

Lesson: Meet halfway or take turns driving long-distance to see each other.

3. He seemed smart and charming from our texting exchange, but he slipped in some perverted comments every so often. I was weirded out but thought it was just his unique sense of humor. I asked to talk to him on the phone briefly before meeting, and he was respectful and sweet during our conversation. I was relieved and eager to meet him, but while I waited at the bar, he started texting vulgar and inappropriate comments. He described what I was wearing, but I didn't see him anywhere. I knew he was watching me, and I freaked out and left. He continued to text me descriptive sexual things he wanted to do to me until I got home and blocked his number.

Lesson: Don't ignore perverted comments.

4. He sent me a message saying he was running late, so I waited by the front door of the dark, crowded bar. We had never met, so I wanted to make sure we found each other before heading in. Twenty minutes went by, so I asked if he was almost there. He said he was looking for parking and would be there soon. Another twenty minutes went by, and he texted me, saying he was on his way. This went on for the next two hours. He continued to send me messages saying he was almost there, and I stupidly waited outside for a guy who never showed up. I should've gone into the bar without him.

Lesson: Enjoy your evening instead of waiting around for a date.

LOCKING EYES DURING INTIMATE MOMENTS IS SO ROMANTIC

When I first moved to Chicago, I went on tons of online dates to meet guys. Online dating was becoming popular, and it was the "cool" way to date at that time, mainly because it was such a new phenomenon.

Pete and I talked briefly to coordinate our meeting place, and then we met later that night at a coffee shop. He was average-looking with a definite aura of geekiness. We talked about movies and TV, and he kept bringing *Star Wars* and *Star Trek* into the conversation, which I knew nothing about. I had seen the movie *Spaceballs* multiple times, but that's as far as my knowledge went. We finished our drinks and agreed to go on a walk. I had made up my mind about him and didn't think I'd see him again, but I wanted to give it a little while longer just to be sure.

The temperature abruptly dropped, causing a chill in the air. I was prepared with a jacket, but he was only wearing a t-shirt. Pete asked if we could stop at his apartment so he could get a coat, and I said sure. He seemed harmless, but as I followed him up the stairs in his building, I texted my friend his address to be safe. She knew I was on a date, and if something happened to me, she knew where I'd be. (I recommend telling at least one trustworthy person the details of your online date—the person's name, where you're going, and when you'll be there—in advance of your date. It's important to protect yourself before meeting a stranger. There are lots of crazies out there!)

I stepped into his apartment, and it was undoubtedly the home of a nerd. I followed him into his room, and he pointed out his *Star Wars* collectibles on the bookshelf. I walked over to get a closer look and saw hundreds of figurines. He said he was going to the bathroom, so I stood there looking at his bookshelf for a few minutes.

I suddenly got an eerie feeling that someone was watching me, so I turned around and found Pete standing by the door, staring at me intensely, and masturbating. I stood there in shock and stared right back at him. I didn't make a sound, probably because no words could justify what I was feeling. Our eyes stayed locked on each other as he silently ejaculated into his hand. He went to get a tissue, and that was my chance to escape the madness! I told him it was nice meeting him and ran out of there.

You might ask why the hell I didn't run as soon as I saw his penis hanging out of his pants, but my legs were glued to the floor. It didn't seem like real life. I was young and naive and didn't know what to do, so I just stood there and watched him masturbate.

I've unfortunately had some online dates where I felt terrified, but my date with Pete wasn't one of them. It was the first strange ending to an online date, but at least I didn't feel uneasy or scared. It was just bizarre, and it was the first of many strange interactions I've had from online dating.

My takeaway: Online dating is full of freaks and nutcases. You have to weed out a lot of losers to find a winner.

SUMMARY

Make sure your dating profile shows the best and truest representation of who you are. Have a variety of pictures and write a short bio. Don't take any communication with guys too seriously, but pay attention to odd messages or red flags early on. If you feel comfortable and want to proceed with a date, try to meet in person as soon as possible. Protect yourself and your safety by meeting in a public place.

CHAPTER 3
GET AWAY FROM ME!

Remember when you walked into the lunchroom in high school, and you saw all the different cliques hanging out in separate areas? There were the popular kids, the jocks, the nerds, the druggies, the goth/emo kids, the theater/music kids, the loners, the normal kids, and the leftovers. Whatever section you migrated to was your pick of where you thought you belonged.

Walking into a room as an adult isn't much different than high school. You survey the people and decide where you'd most fit in. You stick with your crew and don't associate with "different" types. This also relates to dating. You won't approach a guy who doesn't seem to be your type, and if he approaches you, you smile kindly and walk away.

I challenge you to give everyone a chance. You may surprise yourself and fall in love with a guy you'd normally ignore. Appearances can be deceiving. If you judge people based on looks and assume they're not your type before getting to know them, you could pass up an amazing guy.

Miss Girl Next Door meets Mr. Punk Rocker

I went to an off-off-Broadway play in New York City one summer when I was working for a talent agent. I got a free ticket to an obscure play, so I decided to check it out. The theater was mostly empty, so I chose an aisle seat near the back, in case I had to make a quick getaway (I usually prefer to sit front and center for plays so I can see the actors' facial expressions, but I didn't feel like it was appropriate this time).

I noticed Ron instantly. He had spiked bright blue hair, lots of piercings and tattoos covering his body, and multiple chains around his neck and waist. We made eye contact, and then I averted my eyes. I'll admit that I totally judged him at first glance. From my peripheral vision, I saw him walk confidently toward me, and he stopped at my row and asked if he could sit with me. I was new to the city and didn't know anyone, so I meekly said yes.

I'm not sure what I was expecting, but he ended up being a superb guy. His close friend was in the play, so he was there to support her. I was appreciative of his ballsy move for many reasons. First of all, the play wasn't too riveting, and he kept whispering silly comments in my ear. Also, he invited me out for drinks with the cast afterward. I felt like a real New Yorker having drinks out at a bar! It was a weeknight, and I was shocked at how crowded the city was. Although I grew up in big cities, I had never experienced a true nightlife like New York City until that night.

We ended up dating for the summer until I moved away. Anyone that passed us on the street must've thought we were completely mismatched. I had a "girl next door" vibe, sweet and innocent. He looked like a punk rocker from a heavy metal band. I expected someone who dressed that way to be a drug addict, but he didn't smoke or do drugs at all. He was as kind and well-mannered as could be, and I grew to like him a lot.

We bonded over our mutual love of theater, and he took me to all the best spots of New York City. One day I asked him why he had come up to me that night at the theater, and he said it looked like I could use some company. That decision led to an outstanding result. I had the best summer of my young adult life, and I felt a real connection with a guy I'd never normally consider a dating prospect.

My takeaway: Never make assumptions about someone. Ron looked like the complete opposite of me in every way, and I had always avoided guys with his appearance in the past. Luckily, we had similar personalities and connected on many levels. If I had declined his invitation to sit with me at the theater, I wouldn't have experienced a spectacular summer romance with a sensational guy.

MAY I PLEASE USE THE BATHROOM?

I was new to Chicago, and my cousin excitedly called me one day saying he had a friend to set me up with. I was willing to meet someone new, especially a guy my cousin could vouch for. His name was Andrew, and he was a successful stockbroker. He looked extremely handsome in the picture, and I was told that we had similar backgrounds.

When I met Andrew in person a few days later, he seemed like my exact type. I was instantly attracted to him, and I couldn't wait to learn everything about him. We went to a fancy restaurant for dinner, and then he invited me back to his condo to watch a movie. I would never normally agree to go to a stranger's place on the first date. However, since my cousin was friends with Andrew and knew where he lived, I thought it was safe.

His condo was breathtaking. Exquisitely designed with gorgeous furniture, and in an upscale building. We sat on his luxurious sofa and talked for a while. When there was an awkward pause in our conversation, he reached for the remote to find something to watch. He flipped through the channels and then stopped when he saw that the movie *Lolita* was about to start. He joyfully said it was his favorite movie, so I agreed to watch it. I had never heard of it, but I soon discovered that it was about a pedophile! Strange choice for a favorite movie, huh? *Lolita* had an interesting plot, so I was at least entertained by it.

After the movie ended, I asked to use the bathroom, and this is where things took a peculiar turn. Perhaps he was in a frisky mood after watching the sexual interactions between a man and a fourteen-year-old girl? Or maybe watching his favorite movie brought out his devious nature? Whatever the case, I wasn't expecting a simple bathroom visit to turn into a memorable experience. Here's what happened:

Me: "Can I use your bathroom?"

Andrew: "Sure. It's right through there."

He pointed to a door across the living room, and I started walking in that direction.

Andrew: "Wait!" He jumped up and appeared right in front of me. "Will you pee on me instead? I've always wanted someone to pee on me."

Me: My mouth dropped, and I stood there frozen.

Andrew: "Please! It'll be awesome. No one is watching or judging you."

Me: "Uhhhh…"

Andrew: In a pleading tone, "Come on. I feel so comfortable and free around you."

Me: The immediate shock wore off, and my mind rapidly churned with various thoughts. 1. *What the hell is wrong with this weirdo?* 2. *Should I just do it and get it over with?* 3. *I really have to pee.* 4. *Should I grab my purse and run out of here?* 5. *Maybe I'll end up enjoying it.* 6. *Will he ask me to shit on him next?* 7. *I still really have to pee.* 8. *Will* *he like the taste if it gets in his mouth?* 9. *Does he consider this foreplay?* 10. *I have to make a decision.*

Andrew: He sensed my hesitation and assumed that meant I agreed to pee on him. He sprawled out on the carpeted floor right at my feet and lifted his shirt.

Me: As an innocent and inexperienced woman, I figured I'd give it a try. I thought, *Who knows, maybe this will become my fetish!* I stood over him with my legs on either side of his torso and slowly pulled down my pants. I got in a squat position and stared down into his hungry eyes. My bladder was so full and ready to burst at this point, but I couldn't manage to let out even a drop of urine. I waited a few more seconds, then shook my head and said, "I'm sorry; it's not gonna happen." I pulled up my pants, went to the bathroom, and let it all gush out of me into the toilet.

When I came back to the living room, he was sitting on the sofa looking defeated. We both knew that there was nothing more to be said or done. I thanked him for dinner and left. We never spoke again. Looking back on that night, I will say that I never felt scared or unsafe. Luckily, he was a complete gentleman. Even when he asked me to pee on him, he didn't force me or yell or use violence. He simply made a request, and I couldn't do it (not for lack of trying). It's absurd that he asked me to pee on him, which I consider a sexual act, yet we never hugged or kissed or did anything remotely sexual the whole night.

My takeaway: A guy with a nice condo, good friends, and a successful career could be a complete screwball. Even if your friend or relative sets you up, they don't know what he's like when you're alone with him. My cousin thought Andrew would be my ideal match. Maybe he *was* on paper, but there's more to a relationship than what's on a checklist.

Summary

Don't make assumptions about a guy based on his looks or background. You have to give everyone an equal chance. You might become attracted to a guy who isn't your usual type, or you may discover that perfect on paper does not mean perfect for you. Experimenting with a partner can be fun and healthy, but consider saving that for when you're in a committed relationship.

CHAPTER 4

TO KISS OR NOT TO KISS? THAT IS THE QUESTION.

Congrats! You got a first date with a phenomenal guy! It's great to be enthusiastic and jump for joy, but it can also be exhausting, especially if you go on date after date with no success. Here are some dating tips to follow to have a successful experience:

BEFORE YOUR DATE

1. If he's someone you met online, you can do a little digging to make sure he's a real person. Search the internet, and check out his background, age, job, and anything else to make you feel comfortable.

2. If you have mutual friends, you can ask other people what he's like and urge them to share anything you should be cautious of.

3. Agree to meet on a day that's fitting with your schedule. If you know you'll be working late all week and then make a date Friday night when you're exhausted, you won't be the best version of yourself.

4. Try not to go out drinking or partying the night before your date. Even if you feel pumped up, you'll look worn out.

5. Make sure you're well-rested and relaxed. If you had a stressful day leading up to the date, take some time to meditate, go for a peaceful walk, or follow a personal ritual to let go of your anxiety.

6. Take a shower and fix your hair. Start getting ready on the early side so you're not running late and rushing to get it all done.

7. Find out what type of place you're going to. If it's a fancy restaurant, your outfit will be different than if it's a hike in the woods.

8. No matter what type of outfit you wear, it should be clean and fashionable.

9. Tidy up your living space and clean your car if there's a chance that he'll see them.

10. Think of some open-ended questions to ask him if there's ever a pause in the conversation.

MY OPINION ON GOING TO A MOVIE FOR A FIRST DATE

Going to a movie or concert is one of the worst first date ideas if there's nothing else planned afterward. When you're watching a movie, you can't interact or get to know each other at all. However, if you go out to eat to discuss the movie afterward, then it gives you something to talk about in case you're having difficulty making conversation. The reason dinner is not the best idea before the movie is because you may have a miserable time, and then it'll ruin your enjoyment of the movie.

A BETTER FIRST DATE IDEA

If you haven't met in person yet, then stick to a place where you have a quick, easy getaway if necessary. A coffee shop is safe and simple. If you already know the guy and want to make a good impression, you can take it up a notch by meeting for drinks or dinner. Or you can do something active, like going for a walk or playing a sport together. Meet in a public place that's convenient for both of you.

DURING YOUR DATE

Did you know that when you're first getting to know a new potential dating partner, his initial impression of you is based 55% on your appearance and body language, 38% on your style of speaking, and only 7% on what you say? That's why looking your best is important. If you're attracted to him, your body language will show that, and he'll be more interested in you as well. Your speaking style says a lot about your personality, and if you're happy to be there, it will come through in your voice.

1. Have a positive attitude. The date is supposed to be fun, so smile often and enjoy getting to know a new person.

2. Make eye contact. You can flirt just by looking into each other's eyes. It's a subtle yet intense way to grow a connection without speaking.

3. Keep the conversation light. You don't have to only talk about superficial stuff, but avoid heavy topics for the first date.

4. When he's speaking, don't interrupt. Listen and show interest in what he's saying, and ask follow-up questions if you'd like.

5. When you're speaking, keep your voice positive and upbeat. You want to have energy when you speak and avoid any negativity.

6. Try to have an equal balance between talking and listening. The purpose of the date is to share your personalities and discover if you're compatible.

7. Be yourself. If you hide who you are on a first date, you'll have to keep faking it for the rest of the relationship.

8. Add a bit of humor to the conversation. Making jokes will lighten the mood if you're nervous or if you run out of topics to discuss.

9. Stay present. If you start analyzing all his behaviors and comments, you'll miss what he's saying. You can analyze it all when you're alone.

10. Be friendly and polite. You're taking a chance on each other and learning if you want to keep dating, so there's no need to be rude.

MAKING CONVERSATION

If you genuinely like the guy you're on a date with, you may be tempted to talk all about yourself and gush about your lovely life. Or, on the other end of the spectrum, you may ask hundreds of questions to learn only about him. Both of these methods are *bad*. It's best to let the conversation flow. There should be a give and take throughout the date, where you reveal one thing about yourself, and then he says something of equal value.

If you only talk about yourself, your date may get bored and annoyed that you don't seem to care about his life at all. On the other hand, asking tons of questions may feel like a job interview for him. It's acceptable to ask questions, but try to stick to open-ended ones (questions that require more than a yes or no response or a specific piece of information).

Pay attention to your date. If his eyes start to glaze over, change the subject, or ask a question that'll pique his interest.

Be courteous to everyone, not just your date. He will notice how you treat waiters and strangers. Don't whine or complain about anything, and keep an open mind throughout the date.

WHAT ABOUT A GOODBYE KISS?

If you felt chemistry with the guy, a short and sweet goodbye kiss could be a terrific ending to your date. Some people don't believe in kissing on a first date, and I respect that. If the guy leans in for an unwelcome kiss, you can either turn your head and have him plant it on your cheek or avoid his lips and hug him instead.

AFTER YOUR DATE

1. The first thing you should do is ask yourself how you felt about the date. It might be clear that you felt lots of chemistry or felt nothing. Or you may be unsure, which is why this step is important.

2. Over the next 24 hours, you should process your feelings. Do you find yourself smiling every time you think about him? Or do you feel sick and shudder at the thought of seeing him again? If you're still unsure, don't rule him out just yet. You may need to get to know him better to make a decision.

3. Now, you can analyze all his behaviors and comments. Did he say or do anything that sticks out in your mind? Are there any red flags that pop up? If he said one thing that bothered you, but it's not quite a

deal-breaker, are you willing to give him a chance to defend himself and explain why he said it?

4. As tempting as it may be to contact him first, DO NOT DO THAT. While you go through your steps post-date, he has his own ritual that he needs to follow at his own pace. Even if you were the one to ask him out, he needs to be a man and pursue you from now on. If he doesn't ask you out again, he's not interested.

No matter who initiated the first date, the second date should always come from the man. I've made the mistake of asking guys out for not just first dates, but second, third, fourth, and more. The problem with this is that it shifts the male-female dynamic. I'm a feminist and believe in females taking charge and asking for what we want. However, when it comes to dating, when I take charge, it signals the guy to take a backseat in the relationship and grow lazy. He'll expect me to make all the plans and continue to pursue him. He'll never get that power back, and he'll likely grow bored in the relationship and eventually leave.

If you tend to dominate in relationships and prefer to be the one who leads, then becoming equal planning partners after a few dates could be an excellent compromise. You should still allow the guy to pursue you to feel masculine; meanwhile, your leadership role will start to reveal itself.

I'm sorry to say that if you felt that the first date was magnificent, but you never hear from him again, you need to let it go. **He's not for you.**

If he contacts you and you know for sure that you're not interested, don't string him along. Give a gentle rejection. Ignoring him after he asks you out is just mean. The only time I don't respond to a guy when he asks me out for a second date is when he waits a month to contact me again. It makes me wonder, *Did he go out with ten other women in the meantime and then decide he'd settle for me?*

Some guys might prefer that you don't respond, but I like to be upfront and honest. I've gotten a whole variety of negative replies when I tell them we're not compatible, including guys yelling at me, hanging up on me, listing off all my terrible traits, and calling me a lesbian. If nothing else, it makes me extra confident in my decision to never see them again.

If he contacts you for a second date and you *are* interested, then you're on your way to success! If you're still on the fence about him, I'd recommend agreeing to another date to assess your feelings further.

A NIGHT OF FIRSTS...

I was fifteen years old and had spent all my free time for the past few weeks talking on the phone with Will, a boy I met at a party. I had a huge crush on him and was anxious to go on a date with him, which would be my first real date. The Jewish holiday of Purim was coming up, which is a festive gathering where everyone dresses up in costumes and celebrates the saving of the Jewish people. My parents heard me talking about Will incessantly, so they said I could invite him to our synagogue, even though he wasn't Jewish.

My mom picked up Will on the way, and my dad met us at the synagogue for the celebration. I had a marvelous time sitting next to Will and sharing the festivities with someone who had no experience with the Jewish religion. My whole body felt tingly all night, and although I didn't understand the term "sexual tension," that's precisely what I was feeling.

Will must have felt it too because the second we got back to my mom's car and sat down, he started caressing my leg. That hastily evolved to his hands moving up my body and rubbing my breasts. It wasn't exactly pleasurable since there was a layer of fabric in the way, but it was my first experience with a guy touching my chest, or anything else, for that matter.

I could tell that Will wanted to make the most of our short car ride, so he didn't waste any time. Soon after he started touching my breasts, he leaned in and kissed me. It was my first kiss! But he didn't stop there. He kept his lips pressed against mine for the next fifteen minutes and moved his hands under my shirt so they were touching my skin.

I was so engrossed in our make-out session that the rest of the world melted away. I don't know if I particularly enjoyed it, but it was still exhilarating having my first sexual experience with a boy I had a crush on. I heard a car honk in the distance and snapped back to reality. I glanced at my mom and saw her gleaming eyes staring at me through the rearview mirror. *Oh shit!* I thought to myself. My mom just witnessed my first kiss. And my first make-out session. And the first time a guy touched my breasts.

Will sensed a pause in our kissing session, so he decided to ask my mom if he could come over and hang out in my room for a few hours. My mom sternly said, "NO!" Will tried to kiss me again, but I pulled away this time and brushed his hands away from my body. We dropped him off and had a silent ride home. I felt ecstatic for having my first kiss but also revolted knowing my mom had been watching. To add to my uncomfortable feelings, my mom came to my room later that night and had "the talk" with me.

Will called me the next day to discuss our first date. We agreed that it was fantastic, but my feelings of embarrassment took over my excitement about that night. We talked a few more times on the phone, but I kept picturing my mom's glaring eyes whenever I thought about Will.

My takeaway: I definitely had a memorable night of firsts. I had my first date, my first kiss, the first time a guy touched my breasts, and the dreaded sex talk with my mom. I never had a second date with Will, but at least I had my first experience of being interested in a guy who liked me back.

SUMMARY

Put in effort as you prepare for every first date, and go into it with a positive attitude and interest to learn about a new guy. Show off the best version of yourself, and try to have an enjoyable experience. Take time after the date to process your feelings and decide if this is someone you want to continue dating.

CHAPTER 5

WHY DO ALL MY FRIENDS HATE YOU?

You start dating a new guy and invite him along to hang out with your friends on Saturday night. He's intelligent and attractive, and you just know your friends are going to love him. He has a few drinks and makes conversation with everyone. After two hours, he leaves, and you ask what they all thought of him.

They try to be nice, but you can tell that they were put off by him. After convincing them to give an honest opinion, they admit that he was obnoxious and vulgar. You stand up for him and say that he must've been nervous, and then you file their comments away in the back of your mind.

You continue dating him for a few months, and you even consider moving in with him. You slowly start to notice what your friends were talking about, but you want to prove them wrong and show the world that he's a sensational guy. Right after proclaiming your love for him, you find out through the grapevine that he has been sleeping with someone else. You dump him and vow to listen to your friends next time.

When you discover red flags on your own, you're more likely to walk away from the guy and never look back. It's harder when your friends tell you he's wrong for you. You want their approval, and if they give you some negative feedback, your instinct is to get defensive and ignore what they say. I've disregarded friends' opinions of guys I dated, only to realize they were absolutely right, often after months of heartache and misery.

Being the friend who has to tell them the cold, hard truth is also a difficult task. You run the risk of losing their friendship. Hopefully, they'll make their way back to you after understanding that you just wanted the best for them.

I've had many first dates that showed clear red flags, and I internally crossed them off my list of potential boyfriends within the first ten minutes. If a guy does any of these, do not see him again. The same applies to you. Don't be surprised if you never hear from a guy again after you do one or more things on this list.

COMMON RED FLAGS ON A FIRST DATE

1. He shows up remarkably late without an explanation or apology.

2. He orders for you without asking what you want.

3. He talks about himself the whole time and doesn't seem interested in learning about you.

4. He barely speaks at all, so you have to fill the awkward silence.

5. He constantly looks at his phone and texts other people.

6. He's negative or angry without having a good reason.

7. He gets overly emotional and cries to you about a personal problem.

8. He bores you to death, and you find yourself glancing at the clock frequently.

9. He has no concern for your safety.

10. He gets completely drunk.

11. He embarrasses you.

12. He's rude to the waiter or strangers you pass on the street.

13. He trash-talks his ex.

14. He talks about how he hates his family.

15. He agrees with everything you say and has no differing opinions.

All of these are general red flags, but you'll know on your date if he says or does something questionable. Your friends won't always be there to warn you, so it's important for you to remove your blinders and see him clearly. Sometimes he'll hide any red flags on a first date because he's trying to impress you, but his true colors will shine through eventually.

A DATE WITH MR. NON-INCREDIBLE

Doug begged me to go out for weeks, and I finally agreed. I had met him a few times through friends, and I wasn't impressed with his looks or personality. I still decided to give him a fair chance.

This date ended up being the epitome of what NOT to do on a first date. Here is a list of what happened:

1. He showed up an hour late. He insisted on picking me up, so I went outside when he said he was there. He blamed the late arrival on the traffic (which is typical for Los Angeles), and then he spent thirty minutes circling the neighborhood looking for

parking. We were planning on driving somewhere for our date, so it didn't make sense why he parked at all.

2. He had a bad cold. As a germaphobe, I tend to avoid sick people. I asked why he didn't cancel if he was sick, and he said he didn't have a temperature anymore and felt healthy enough for our date. He was coughing and sneezing the whole night, and I was utterly appalled.

3. He was wearing old, dirty, tattered clothing, and his hair was greasy and unkempt. I knew he had a lucrative job, and I had seen him wear suits in other encounters with him. It almost seemed like he was trying to be as unimpressive as possible.

4. His car was a total disaster. We literally walked a mile to get to his car in the summer heat, and his car was the nastiest piece of junk I had ever seen. It was at least thirty years old and falling apart, and the two back windows were broken. He warned me that a squirrel had made a home for itself in his car, so it had a slight animal smell. When I got in, I smelled a mix of urine, vomit, and weed, which made me want to barf. He said the broken windows would air out the smell, and of course, the air conditioner was broken, which added to my repulsion. I told him I would be glad to drive, but he wouldn't let me.

5. He had no plans for our date, despite telling me in advance that he had our whole night figured out. I suggested the Grove, which is an area with shops, restaurants, and a movie theater, and he liked that idea.

6. He refused to use the paid parking lot, so he spent twenty minutes driving around side streets until he finally found a free spot.

7. I was starving and asked if we could go somewhere to eat. He didn't have an opinion on what type of food, but when I pointed out different restaurants and cafes, he vetoed all my options.

8. We agreed on an Italian place, and as soon as we sat down, he ordered appetizers for us without asking if that's what I wanted. He also ordered a pitcher of beer and said, "one glass." He didn't give me the chance to order a drink for myself.

9. He oozed negativity. Along with coughing and sneezing, he was not an optimistic person. He had a permanent frown on his face, and he didn't even try to make conversation. I asked questions to get to know him, and he gave one-word answers without asking me anything in return.

10. He was rude to the waiter. I tried being extra kind and friendly to make up for his bad behavior, but the waiter was still offended.

11. He pulled out his phone after the menus were taken away, and he hunched over and stared at it until the food came.

12. Talking to him was like pulling teeth, so I gave up and stared at the clock on the wall, praying for time to speed up.

13. He ate like a pig. While I elegantly cut my food into little pieces, he shoved it all into his mouth, letting sauce and food particles go flying everywhere.

14. He ordered a second pitcher of beer for himself and was completely wasted by the end of the meal.

15. When the check arrived, he realized that he left his wallet at home. I paid for the meal, and he promised

to pay me back on our next date. (Yeah, right! No way was a second date ever happening.)

16. As much as I wanted to end our miserable date right then, I didn't want to get in the car with a drunk driver. I had free passes to the movie theater in that complex, so I chose a romantic comedy that I was interested in seeing.

17. Walking back to his car, we passed a group of sketchy guys. I was afraid of what the guys would do, but he was oblivious to our surroundings and didn't pick up his pace at all.

18. We made it safely back to his car and had a silent ride home.

19. He asked if he could come up to my apartment, and I firmly said no.

20. As he pulled up in front of my place, he leaned in to kiss me. I pretended not to notice, jumped out of the car, and said thanks for dropping me off.

My takeaway: Every single thing about my date with Doug was a red flag. It shocked me how one person could break every rule in dating, but he accomplished it. If I had ended the date as soon as I learned he was sick, I would've saved myself from an evening of red flags. Lesson learned!

SWIMMING WITH GIRLS IS A NO-NO

My first date with Chris was delightful. He took me to an ice cream parlor (my favorite first-date spot), and we clicked instantly. We had so much in common, and we spent hours talking, laughing, and inching toward each other to get a sense of each other's energy. At the end of the night, he gave me a quick peck on the cheek and said goodbye.

Chris told me that he was a swimmer in high school, so I invited him to my community pool for our second date. We first had some riveting conversation, and then we went to separate rooms to change. I knew he was interested in me when he walked out in his bathing suit with an erection. I pretended not to notice and instead turned away and laughed to myself.

We both jumped in the pool and had a blast flirting and splashing each other. He made a side comment about how he wasn't allowed to swim with girls growing up. I asked why, and he said he grew up in an immensely religious home. I asked some follow-up questions, but Chris reassured me that he wasn't religious anymore. We moved on to other topics, and I pushed that fact out of my mind.

The rest of the date was marvelous! After swimming, we ate lunch and bonded more. I felt intense chemistry between us, and I couldn't wait to learn everything about him. Unfortunately, he was about to visit his parents in Michigan, and he wouldn't be back for three weeks. He promised to keep in touch, and we said goodbye after another terrific time.

Chris kept his word. I was worried that the three weeks would drag on without him, but they flew by! Chris messaged me regularly, and we had long, deep discussions that went on all night. We told each other secrets and fears and life goals, and I felt like he was "the one."

Sadly, as soon as he got back in town, he disappeared from my life. I didn't understand what went wrong. I overanalyzed all our conversations and wondered what I said that could've pushed him away. I didn't sleep for weeks as I tried to come up with a logical explanation for his disappearance.

In most cases, when a guy ghosts me, I don't get the satisfaction of learning why. However, Chris popped back into my life a few years later. I had already moved out of state, but he sent me a long message apologizing for his behavior. He explained that his religious upbringing made him freak out about seeing me again. He was attracted to me but had zero experience with women. He assumed I'd want to be with a more experienced man, so he got scared and disappeared.

My takeaway: I appreciated his honesty, even though it was years later. I knew it took courage for him to admit that to me. I realized my mistake in pushing away his comment about being religious. It was a red flag that I ignored, but I should've paid attention to it. I assumed he had moved on from those beliefs, but you can't escape your past. It's a part of you, just like it was a part of him. Visiting his parents probably reinforced his religious beliefs, and he felt guilty for betraying them by swimming with me "in sin."

SUMMARY

Don't ignore red flags or feedback from others. If you notice that something the guy says or does on your date makes you uncomfortable, get more information about it. If there are obvious red flags on your date, don't waste another second on him. And if *you* show any red flags, you shouldn't be surprised if you never hear from him again. Remember, it goes both ways.

CHAPTER 6

YOU LOVE MUSICAL THEATER, TOO?

From a young age, I was involved in musical theater. I started when I was ten and then performed in many musicals throughout my teenage years. I developed a crush on a few guys per show, but I never pursued them because I was young and didn't truly understand what flirting even meant. As I got older and realized that musical theater attracts only a few straight men, it was no surprise that all the men I had crushes on ended up being gay.

I had a huge crush on a musical theater guy in high school, but he had a girlfriend for three years. He was cute, and she was not attractive at all. I didn't understand why he was dating her, but when I saw him making out with his new boyfriend a few years later, it suddenly clicked that he wasn't attracted to females at all. I vowed to never be a woman who is in a long-term relationship with a man who is unsure of his sexuality.

Before continuing, I'd just like to say that I'm LGBTQ-friendly. I went to Ithaca College, which is ranked as one of the top LGBTQ-inclusive schools in the country. I have plenty of friends in all of those categories, and I coached multiple people in those categories as well. My theater interest happens to attract mainly gay men to the stage, so I've accepted that as reality.

However, I'd like the men I date to be unquestionably straight. I don't think that's too high of a standard. And because I grew up surrounded by many gay men, I came to have pretty accurate "gaydar." Four percent of people identify as LGBTQ, and there are presumably many more who either don't say or don't know yet. That means that if I go on 20 dates with 20 different guys, there's a chance that one of them will be gay or unsure of his sexuality.

For some reason, guys feel genuinely comfortable pouring out their life stories to me, even on first dates. I've heard so many strange things that nothing shocks me, so when they see my non-judgmental face, they continue sharing secrets. Guys have amazingly revealed that they either fantasize about being with men, or find men more attractive than women, or sometimes engage in same-sex activity.

STUCK IN THE CLOSET

One guy I dated admitted that his parents sent him to therapy for five years because he told them he was gay, but they wanted him to "get the gay out." I was the first woman he went out with, but he officially announced that he was gay soon after.

Another guy I went out with told me his mom was the only family he had left. She desperately wanted him to have kids, so he dated women to please her. He showed zero interest in me, but as soon as we walked by a male friend of his, his eyes lit up, and he got a pep in his step. They heavily flirted with each other in front of me, and I felt like the third wheel on my own date. A love connection was surely made that day, but not with me!

I felt sad for these guys. They lived their lives hiding from the truth. They wanted to be accepted by their parents and friends, so they lied about who they were and wanted to be with. The coach part of me wanted to help them, but it wasn't my place to do that. I couldn't date them anymore because it was clear to both of us that we were looking for different things—or technically, the same thing! We both wanted men. They just needed the confidence to admit that to themselves and the world.

DOES DINING AT A FANCY RESTAURANT EQUAL A PROPOSAL?

I had a friend named Amanda who was dating Michael for a few years, and she thought he'd for sure propose soon. She was head over heels in love with him and told me she had found her soulmate. I was thrilled for her, and she enthusiastically called me one day saying this was going to be the night! Michael was taking her to a fancy restaurant, and she knew he was going to ask her to be his wife.

I waited impatiently by the phone, but when I got the call, Amanda was bawling and mumbling phrases I couldn't understand. When her words finally made sense, my stomach dropped. He didn't propose. He didn't want to date her anymore. In fact, he didn't want to date *women* anymore. He wanted to *be* a woman. He felt the need to break the news to her in a fancy restaurant. They broke up, and he got gender confirmation surgery to become the woman he always wanted to be.

My takeaway: I felt awful for Amanda, but I also felt sad for Michael (who became Michelle). Michelle was stuck in the wrong gender for so long, and she finally faced her truth, luckily before marrying someone she wasn't sexually attracted to anymore. It would've been a lot more complicated if they had gotten married before Michelle admitted it to herself and Amanda. Although it was a devastating time for both of them, they were soon free to live their own lives and find partners they both wanted.

SUMMARY

If you are sure you're straight, then you want to make sure the guy you're dating is also straight. If he seems unsure of his sexuality, you'll always worry that he's going to leave you for a man.

Chapter 7

YOU WANT TO HAVE KIDS WITH ME AFTER ONE DATE?

You just graduated college, moved to a popular city, and found a job in your field. A mature, handsome guy asks you out, and you gladly accept his invitation. On the date, you ask him about himself, and he skips the small talk and gets straight to the point. He's 35 and sick of being single. He wants to be married and have two kids by the time he's 37.

It doesn't take a math genius to figure out that he essentially wants to get married immediately for his ideal timeline to play out accurately. As a 22-year-old recent college graduate, the idea of marriage right now is absurd. You just aren't ready for that type of commitment. You want to have a few years of adventures before settling down and having kids.

Fast forward ten years, and you're still single and now desperately searching for a partner who wants to be married and have two kids within the next few years. Although you blew off the 35-year-old all those years ago for being direct on your date, you find yourself being just as direct on first dates. You keep discovering that these guys are in a different stage of life and not ready for a real commitment.

At first, you weren't ready, and now you can't find any marriage-minded guys. What's going on here?

Psychologist Daniel Levinson developed the "Seasons of Life" theory that identifies different stages of life that adults go through:

1. **Early Adult Transition (Ages 17–22):** You become an adult and choose to attend college or enter the workforce. You may leave home and begin your first serious relationship.

2. **Entering the Adult World (Ages 22–28):** You start to make more decisions about who you are, what you want to do, and what you value in life.

3. **Age 30 Transition (Ages 28–33):** You could have major lifestyle changes at this stage, like getting married or having kids.

4. **Settling Down (Ages 33–40):** You begin to establish a routine, reach goals, and behave like a mature adult. You may already be a parent and have more responsibilities in life.

5. **Mid-Life Transition (Ages 40–45):** You evaluate your life and may change your values and your vision of the future. You could get divorced or change careers during this time.

6. **Entering Middle Adulthood (Ages 45–50):** You start to make choices about your future and think about the legacy you're leaving.

7. **Culmination of Middle Adulthood (Ages 50–60):** You may reach the end of your working life and make plans for retirement.

8. **Late Adulthood (Age 60+):** You reflect on life and think about all the decisions you've made thus far.

When you're 22, you may not be ready to settle down, but then you might feel ready by the time you're 30. Dating someone in a similar stage of life is important so you don't waste each other's time. The age range of each stage isn't exact, but it's critical to confirm that the guy you're dating is in the same stage as you.

MY BABY FACE TRICKS THEM ALL

I've always looked young, so younger guys tend to flock to me. Even relatives that I've known my whole life are shocked to discover my real age. When I graduated from college, my parents' friends thought I was graduating from junior high. I get carded everywhere, even when seeing R-rated movies. I find it amusing when people are so wrong about my age.

It's a little more difficult in the dating world to be thought of as a young girl instead of a mature woman. Teenagers hit on me all the time, and I have to kindly tell them how inappropriate it is. Guys that aren't at the legal age to drive have asked me out. I give them credit for their ballsy approach to dating, but I always decline.

In my mid-20s, I could easily pass for an 18-year-old. In fact, I played a high school student in many TV shows. They loved using me as a background actor because I was of legal age but looked ten years younger. Working in that environment, I got asked out by a variety of guys. If they were there without parental supervision, then they had to be at least 18.

I figured I'd give these guys a chance. Why not? They were at their sexual peak, and I was inexperienced and open to new adventures. The first thing I did was ask to see their license. No way was I going to date an underage guy. After confirming that they were 18, we made plans and started dating!

HERE'S TO YOU, MRS. ROBINSON

One of these 18-year-olds, Charlie, was still in high school. His parents let him date me, but they had no idea that I was 25. When you're older, a seven-year age difference is practically nothing. However, a high school student and young professional are in two different worlds.

He was undoubtedly good-looking, but, growing up in a strict Catholic household, he had zero experience with women. All we did was kiss, and he admitted that I was his first kiss ever. He bragged to his friends that he was dating an older woman, and it promptly got back to his parents. I thankfully never met them. They probably would've shot me if they knew my age. Charlie and I had to stop dating, but it was fun while it lasted.

TIME WARP BACK TO COLLEGE

I also dated Sam when I was 25. He was 18 and just starting college. He felt like the coolest guy on campus for dating an older woman. He took me to frat parties, and I felt so out of place. Of course, no one knew that I didn't belong, but I knew. Being with him was like a time warp back to my college days. College was a blast, but I didn't fit into that environment anymore. Sam and I dated for a few weeks, but it rapidly dissolved. I just couldn't date high school or college guys anymore.

TIME WARP TO MY FUTURE

Soon after Sam, I met a sophisticated man named David. This time, I was with someone seven years older. I thought this was just what I needed! David was an intelligent, successful entrepreneur who treated me like a queen. He wined and dined me and showed me all the best spots around town. I didn't have to worry about his curfew or take care of his drunk college buddies. He was mature and worldly, and he was a nice change from my past relationships.

I went to a Memorial Day barbecue with David, and he went off to talk to his male friends. I scanned the backyard and instantly felt out of place once again. There were no drunk college kids to take care of, but instead, there were dozens of toddlers running around, causing chaos. Since David was in his 30s, all his friends were married with children. I tried to befriend the women, but they were in deep conversations about pregnancy and raising kids. I had nothing to add.

For a woman whose sole purpose in life is to have kids, David would've been a splendid partner. He was kind and generous, but we weren't a good fit. I didn't feel ready to settle down at that point, while he wanted to start a family right away. We had a long talk about our life goals, and we mutually decided to break up.

My takeaway: Dating someone in high school or college when you're past that point is a waste of time. You're in different stages of life, and you should try to find people closer to your age. The same applies to dating someone much older. If you still want to have adventures, but the other person is ready to get married, you need to discuss that early on.

IS SHE MAKING OUT WITH HER GRANDFATHER?

I was at a party and sat on the couch with a few people. I began chatting with the woman next to me. Her name was Jessica. She was beautiful and charming and told me how she just had a huge party for her 25th birthday. A much older man was sitting next to her, and every so often, he'd whisper something in her ear and make her laugh. He looked like he could be her grandfather, but their interaction was too flirtatious for that.

I got up and mingled with others, and a little while later, I looked over at the couch and saw Jessica making out with that older man. I stared at them in awe. I've seen mismatched couples before, but this was the biggest age gap I'd ever witnessed.

I went back to the couch to find out more details. Jessica told me that they met on a cruise and fell in love. I asked him about his life, and I deduced that he was around 85 years old, based on his stories. I watched them the rest of the night, and they appeared to be genuinely happy with each other.

Jessica was beginning to enter her young adult stage, while he was far into late adulthood. I don't know if she was waiting for him to die to get all his money or if she truly cared about him, but it was the strangest couple I've seen. A 20-year age difference is acceptable if both people are in the same stage of life, but a 60-year difference is ridiculous.

SUMMARY

Figure out what stage of life you're in, and make sure the guy you're dating is in the same stage before taking the relationship to the next level. You don't want to waste your time or his by continuing to date someone in a different stage.

PART TWO

FROM DATING TO DEEPER COMMITMENT

CHAPTER 8
ARE YOU MY BOYFRIEND YET?

You've been hanging out with a guy for the past few weeks. Sometimes he holds your hand and treats you like a queen, while other times, he acts like you're one of his buddies. You're confused as to your relationship status. Does he just want to be friends? Every night ends with a make-out session, but you have no idea if that means anything.

Don't make the mistake of rushing the "boyfriend" status. Just like a guy needs to move at his own pace when he asks you out on a date, he will ideally ask you to be his girlfriend when he feels ready.

Sometimes guys don't care about labels, but if it's important to you, then you should communicate what you want from dating him. If you're on the same page and want to continue hooking up with no expectations for a future relationship, then go right ahead. But if you are looking for a solid partnership while he wants to play the field, then you should move on to find a more compatible match.

COMMON RELATIONSHIP STATUSES

1. **Friends with benefits:** You've been friends for a while, and now you sometimes hook up when you

hang out. You also hang out with clothes on and do "friends" activities if you're not in the mood for sex.

2. **Hookup buddies:** You hooked up right after meeting and have unbelievable physical chemistry. There's not much of an emotional connection, but you continue hooking up because the sex is terrific.

3. **It's complicated:** You may have been friends with benefits or hookup buddies, and one of you wants to take it to the next level. You can't agree on what your status is. Therefore, it's complicated.

4. **Talking:** You basically have a pen pal. You talk regularly through text and maybe even on the phone, but no one is making a move to ask the other out.

5. **Dating:** You've been out a few times, and you like him. You may be dating other guys as well just to keep your options open. If you've had sex with him, you might assume he's only having sex with you. Because you're still in the dating phase, though, he's not breaking any rules by having sex with others.

6. **Open relationship:** This status tends to exist when you put pressure on him to be your boyfriend. He can get around it by asking for an open relationship. Then he'll call you his girlfriend but still be allowed to date and sleep with other women.

7. **Exclusively dating:** You're not quite ready to use the boyfriend/girlfriend terms, but it's essentially the same thing. You're only dating each other and sleeping with each other in this phase.

8. **Boyfriend/girlfriend:** You are officially boyfriend and girlfriend. You're seeing only each other and sleeping only with each other, and you can proudly introduce him to all your friends as your boyfriend.

TIMING IS EVERYTHING

I was dating Corey for a few months. We talked about how we weren't seeing anyone else, so we were in the "exclusively dating" phase for a long time. I wanted him to ask me to be his girlfriend, but he never mentioned it. I tried sending him girlfriend vibes and saying obvious comments about him not being my boyfriend yet, but he never seemed to get the message. I finally gave in one night and asked if he'd be my boyfriend. He said, "Oh, I thought I already was!"

My takeaway: Sometimes, guys are completely clueless about your relationship status. In this case, I didn't rush the boyfriend status. If I had asked him after just a few dates, I probably would've scared him away. I knew we were on the same page and heading in the right direction, so I brought it up at the optimal time.

CURSED AFTER NO NEW YEAR'S KISS

Isaac was raised as an Orthodox Jew. He decided to break out of his shell after college. As a Jewish woman, I thought he was a marvelous match for me. We were attracted to each other, had similar dreams for the future, and both had a love of music and theater.

Little did I know that Isaac was pursuing multiple women at the same time. He wanted to jump into the world of dating full-force, and he didn't put much effort into hiding all his prospects. I soon talked to women who were also dating him, and we started to compete for Isaac's attention. He even invited me to a New Year's Eve party, and at midnight, I caught him making out with someone else.

Our status jumped around from "it's complicated" to "dating" to an "open relationship," but we never made it to the "boyfriend/girlfriend" status, which I desperately longed for.

After a few months, I was worn out from trying to convince him to upgrade our relationship status. He got quite drunk one night, and I broke it off with him right before he passed out. I had always been interested in his housemate, so I made out with him before walking out of their house forever with my head held high.

My takeaway: As soon as I discovered Isaac was playing the field and dating multiple women, I should've ended it. I grew attached to his charismatic personality, but he wasn't interested in being my boyfriend. I dragged our relationship on for much longer than I should have, and I was the one who suffered in the end.

IN THE GAME OF THRONES, THERE ARE NO WINNERS

Joe and I were both new to Portland. We had apartments, but no jobs, no friends, and no idea about our futures. We met at a party and instantly connected. I heard about a Harry Potter pub crawl a few days later, and he was delighted to join me. Although I lived a few miles away from Joe, I spent every second with him. We cooked and went to restaurants together, we slept in his bed every night, we searched for jobs together, and we watched shows together. He introduced me to *Game of Thrones* and caught me up on all the episodes.

As a social butterfly, I went to events to make friends, and he always came with me. People often asked me if he was my boyfriend, but I always said no. This went on for a few months until I finally broke down and asked him, "What are we doing? Are we dating? Are we boyfriend/girlfriend? Are we friends with benefits?"

He responded that he wanted to keep things just as they were. He said, "I don't want to be in a relationship because I just moved here and want to keep my options open. You're the most important person in my life. I need to see you all the time, so let's just continue to be friends." Friends? I thought we were a little more than friends at that point, but I kept my mouth shut.

A few days after that talk, he met a hot girl at a party and then told me he wanted to date other people. Big surprise. I was angry, but my competitive side swiftly emerged. I like to win, so for every date he went on, I went on two. We still saw each other at all times except when we were going on dates with other people. I'd dress in a sexy outfit, stop at his place just to say hi, and then waltz off to a date.

Our "friendship" was becoming utterly unhealthy. We continued to hang out, and I had to constantly deny to myself and everyone else that we were dating. I freaked out about the state of our relationship every two months, but he always had the same response: "I need you in my life, but I don't want you as my girlfriend. Let's just keep things the way they are." A few times, I told him I didn't want to see him ever again, but the most that lasted was a week.

This whole saga went on for nine months, and I was losing my patience. The turning point for me was a camping trip I went on with Joe and some friends. Joe spent the whole weekend flirting like crazy with a girl there. They both knew how I felt about him, but that didn't stop them from going on hikes and sharing intimate moments alone. I got depressed and jealous watching them together, but I knew there was nothing I could do. I was so mad at her and Joe, and on the car ride home, I told Joe that I was cutting off ties with him forever. I couldn't live like this anymore.

That night was the season finale of *Game of Thrones,* and it was fittingly the only episode I watched without Joe. I ran into him a few times after that camping trip, and we had brief, awkward exchanges. I learned that he started dating the girl from the camping trip soon after, and he had no problem using the "girlfriend" label with her.

My takeaway: If a guy leads you on and wants to be "just friends" but still have sex with you, he's not worthy of your time. Joe never wanted to be my boyfriend, and I allowed him to take advantage of me and my interest in him. I kept waiting for him to be ready for a commitment with me, but that never happened. I wasted nine months on a guy who wasn't fully into me.

SUMMARY

When you start dating someone, make sure you both want the relationship to proceed in the same direction. If he keeps making excuses for not wanting to be exclusive with you, then you should move on. Don't make assumptions about your relationship status without having a conversation about it. You might be on the same page without even realizing it.

CHAPTER 9

WHY DON'T WE SEE
EYE TO EYE?

Everyone wants compatibility in a relationship. You may have discovered that you're usually attracted to a guy who's the complete opposite of you, but your odds for sustaining a relationship are much better if you have similarities. You don't need to find a guy with an identical personality to yours, but if you're total opposites in every way, the excitement will soon subside.

The four main types of compatibility are physical, emotional, mental, and spiritual. They're all important and connected to one another. A lack of compatibility in one area will create problems that will spill into other areas of the relationship. It takes time to develop all aspects of compatibility. When you find someone you connect with on all four levels, hold on to this person forever.

PHYSICAL COMPATIBILITY

This type of compatibility is the easiest to find, but it's difficult to maintain. The first time you're intimate with a guy, it's new and exciting, and you get to explore each other's bodies and preferences. Once the novelty wears off, you have to keep working at it to nurture the relationship.

People prefer different types of touch, so it's important to communicate your needs and desires to let the guy know if he's on the right track. Any intimate act, including sex, hugging, and even holding hands, causes an increased production of oxytocin, often called the "love hormone." This increase leads to the release of endorphins, which is your natural pain-killing hormone. It helps relieve stress and increase pleasure.

Physical intimacy seems straightforward, but if your body is not functioning properly, it can have an impact on your relationship. Certain illnesses, diseases, medications, hormonal changes, and aging can affect your sexuality. Everyone reacts differently to medication. Prescription pills for depression or high blood pressure, over-the-counter medicine, and birth control pills can all influence you. Keep that in mind when you're first getting to know someone. Hopefully, the physical compatibility is strong, but if not, there are often ways to work through the issues.

EMOTIONAL COMPATIBILITY

This type of compatibility takes time to develop. Once you feel more comfortable opening up to a partner and sharing your hopes and fears, the emotional connection will grow. It's not necessary to have the same emotional needs, but you should understand the emotional needs of your partner and respond appropriately.

Engaging in activities together and sharing deep, personal stories with each other are wonderful ways to bring you emotionally closer. Talking about your feelings can help you release any insecurities you have about the relationship. If you have blocked emotions, opening up to the incidents that happened in your past can help you get through them for the future.

Your emotions are connected to your heart. If your heart aches for your partner, you probably have excellent emotional compatibility.

MENTAL COMPATIBILITY

Your brain is the most important organ in your body. The body and mind are completely connected, so having a powerful mental connection with a guy can lead to mind-blowing sex. However, if your mind is continuously churning with negative thoughts and ideas, it can ruin your pleasure.

Being able to have an intellectual discussion with your partner can be so satisfying. It can also make your attraction grow tenfold. If you're not on the same mental wavelength, it may be apparent early on in the relationship.

When you grow old together, conversation and mental stimulation will be more important than sex. You want someone who challenges your intellect and keeps you thinking. If the conversation flows and you never get bored with each other, you may be on your way to having incredible mental compatibility.

SPIRITUAL COMPATIBILITY

This type of compatibility includes your religion, beliefs, energy, and soul. It's the hardest to define, yet it is the piece of the puzzle that's missing in many relationships. It's the feeling you have when you've found your soulmate.

All people have an energy that radiates from them. You can discover who you best connect with by paying attention to the interaction between your energy and others. If you're compatible with a guy physically, emotionally, and mentally, but something seems off, you may be lacking spiritual compatibility.

If you're unsure how to assess it, notice your energy level after you've left your date. If you feel alive and energized, there's possible long-term potential. If you feel drained and relieved to be on your own, it's a sign that you aren't spiritually connected.

Having the same religious background and belief in a higher power can help bring you together. It'll make things easier if you want to pass these beliefs on to your children. If that's not a factor, it's still important to feel that your energy is in alignment with his energy. Having spiritual compatibility will make you two unstoppable.

MY BODY IS A TEMPLE

I dated a guy named Brian for over a year. The sex was fabulous at first, but after a while, sex became painful for me. I thought maybe I had an STD, or there was something wrong, but the doctor told me my body was fine. A few more months went by, and I suffered through sex for the sake of our relationship. It wasn't pleasurable anymore, but I didn't understand what was going on.

We eventually broke up, and I was afraid to have sex again for a long time. I finally did, and everything felt amazing! It suddenly clicked with me that the reason sex didn't feel good with Brian was because my body was rejecting his penis. I wasn't into the guy anymore, and my body knew that before my brain did.

My takeaway: Your body is completely connected to your mind. If you don't enjoy the person, you're not going to enjoy the sex. You need to be compatible in all four ways: physical, emotional, mental, and spiritual. If one element of compatibility is lacking, it'll affect the whole relationship. My heart wasn't in it anymore. Once the emotional compatibility died, the physical part went kaput as well.

UNMATCHED PUZZLE PIECES

I dated a guy who wasn't on my level intellectually. I enjoyed playing logic games and having stimulating conversations, but he just wasn't as mentally developed. He was all heart and poured out his emotions to me, but I wanted him to challenge me intellectually.

I was doing a jigsaw puzzle once, and he came over and joined me. I focused on all the edge pieces and speedily created the rectangular border. I then looked over to see his progress and stared in horror at him as he tried to jam two pieces together that clearly didn't fit. It was evident that he processed things differently than I did, and I knew our relationship wouldn't last. We kept dating for a few more months, but we never saw eye to eye on any intellectual issues.

TOO SMART FOR YOUR OWN GOOD

After that guy, I vowed to date a guy with more intellect. I got what I wanted to the extreme! The next guy I dated was a genius. He was by far the smartest person I'd ever met. I could complete a puzzle relatively quickly, but he'd get it done at lightning speed. Playing games competitively with him wasn't enjoyable anymore because he'd win every time, no matter what.

Because he was so intelligent, he lacked in the emotional department. He was able to fake emotions, but I don't know if he ever wholly felt anything. I started to miss the previous guy's level of emotions, and I wondered if I'd ever have both.

I CAN'T PINPOINT WHY IT'S NOT WORKING

I was dating a guy for a while, and everyone thought we were a match made in heaven. We got along well and had similar personalities and interests. Our bodies fit together like two puzzle pieces, and we had deep conversations and challenged each other intellectually. I couldn't put my finger on it, but I felt like something was off between us. I didn't know what it was, and I often cried myself to sleep because it didn't make sense to me why I didn't feel connected to a seemingly perfect man.

I couldn't get past the feeling that something was off, no matter how many people told us we'd unquestionably end up together. I ended the relationship, still confused why I didn't feel like he was my soulmate. Years later, I read a book about needing a spiritual connection with a partner, and it dawned on me that *that* was the missing piece from our relationship. It's impossible to explain, but my intuition told me that we lacked an essential aspect of compatibility.

SUMMARY

It's important to have complete compatibility with a man, and that includes all aspects: physical, emotional, mental, and spiritual. Your relationship can survive without all four, but it may not be as fulfilling as one that has all aspects.

CHAPTER 10
NO RING ON HIS FINGER!

I've heard from numerous men that once they're married, they suddenly get hit on by every woman who walks by. Being taken and unavailable adds to their appeal, and they have to push women away, even if they had never been noticed by anyone before.

It amazes me that women flock toward married men, while I try my hardest to avoid them. Admittedly, after making eye contact with a guy, my eyes instantly go to his left hand to see if there's a ring on his finger. If there is, I avert my eyes and focus on someone else.

GUYS YOU SHOULDN'T DATE OR PURSUE

1. Married guys

2. Engaged guys

3. Guys in a committed relationship

4. Guys who aren't ready for a committed relationship

5. Ex-boyfriends

6. Guys who are closely related to someone you dated

If a guy is married, engaged, or in a serious relationship, you have no right to get involved with him. It's not fair to him, his partner, or you. Maybe his relationship is on the verge of ending, but it's not over yet. As long as he's still committed to someone else, that means he can't focus all his attention and affection on you. Wait until he makes a clean break from his partner before swooping in and taking him.

You'll learn quickly if a guy isn't ready for a committed relationship. If he's newly separated or divorced, he may have tons of baggage to work through, including custody battles and emotional trauma. His ex is likely still in the picture, and she won't rest until he's as miserable as she is. If she calls incessantly while you're on a date, chances are that he hasn't moved on from his past.

Dating an ex-boyfriend can become problematic. You may have shared memorable experiences, but you broke up for a reason. Unless that reason is no longer valid, you'll just fall into the same patterns as the last time you dated. It's a waste of time to expect the relationship to be different this time. The only exception is if you have both made an effort to change and fix what was broken when you were together the first time.

If you date a guy and then start dating his brother soon after, do you expect that to end well? There are millions of single men in the world, so you can easily find someone outside of his family to date. You're not only destroying your relationship with both guys, but it may ruin their sibling bond forever as well.

EMOTIONAL CHEATING TAKES YOU DOWN A DARK PATH

I went to a bar one night with some friends, and I started talking to a guy named Jeremy. He was good-looking and friendly, so my eyes glanced down at his left hand. No wedding ring! Woohoo! I felt like we connected in every way, and I was already envisioning our wedding in my mind. We ignored our friends for the rest of the night and sat in the corner of the bar talking for hours.

I was totally smitten. The bartender announced last call, and we looked around and noticed that hardly anyone else was still there. Then Jeremy said the dreaded word that made my heart sink. He said, "It's getting late, and I have to get up early tomorrow to pick up my wife from the airport." What! He has a *wife*?! How could he do this to me! I just wasted five hours talking to a married guy? Why wasn't he wearing a wedding ring? He asked for my number and said he'd love to hang out again soon. I was numb from disappointment, but I gave it to him and left.

Before continuing the story, I just want to mention that I always check for a wedding ring before flirting with a guy. If he doesn't have a wedding ring on, I pay careful attention to what he says to find out if he has a girlfriend or fiancée. I've wasted lots of precious time talking with unavailable men, and when they slip in the fact that they have a girlfriend after a long, deep conversation, it infuriates me. Jeremy was one of those people. He didn't say one thing about his wife or make it known that he was unavailable until the end of the night. He told me later that he never wore his ring unless he was out with his wife. Isn't the point of wearing it to show the world that you're taken? I'm sure he knew what he was doing, and it made me angry.

I never thought I'd hear from Jeremy again after that splendid night. To my surprise, he texted me a few days later and invited me out for drinks with a group of his friends. After learning that he was married, I had written him off as a dating possibility, but I thought maybe he had some friends that were similar to him and single.

I agreed to meet them, but when I got there, his six friends consisted of three married couples. I asked where his wife was, and he said she didn't like to go out on weeknights. So I was his "date" for the evening. I had my guard up, but I began to relax as the night went on. His friends were welcoming and interested to learn about me, and they didn't mention his wife at all. It almost felt like they wished he wasn't married and would date me instead.

His friends all left, but I stayed late and talked with Jeremy, against my better judgment. He had a few drinks in him and started revealing all these issues he had with his wife. An alarm went off in my head, but I couldn't stop myself from asking tons of questions and learning everything I could about his relationship. I was so conflicted at that point. I wanted to be his love coach and help him repair his relationship, but I also felt a powerful connection to him and wanted him to ditch his wife and be with me!

I soon became his supportive, caring friend. I *hated* being that. I didn't want to be a shoulder to cry on, but I got stuck in that role for a while. I was aware that our friendship wasn't appropriate for many reasons. Besides the fact that he was married, he was also sharing intimate details of his relationship with me, and I felt like he was emotionally cheating on his wife.

As I'm sure you've guessed, that emotional cheating turned into actual cheating. I'm not proud of this. I knew it was wrong and appalling, but I couldn't help myself. I had many strong emotions during my time with him. I had always judged others for cheating, but now I was judging myself. I felt guilty for being "the other woman," and I felt sad that I couldn't tell anyone about my secret romance. Most of all, I felt true love for the first time in my life, but that feeling was mixed with a sickening dread that it would all blow up in my face.

I met his wife a few times, and she was courteous and homely. Every night I dreamed about her watching me from afar, with sorrow in her eyes. I hated that I was destroying her life. Jeremy said she knew about us, even though he never uttered a word about me. He told me that she continually asked him, "Do you love me as much as you love Rachel?" That must have been heartbreaking for him to hear. When I imagined her saying that, it felt like someone punching me hard in the gut. That feeling of being punched in the gut lasted for six months. I barely slept. I barely ate. It felt wonderful and terrible at the same time. I couldn't decide if I was in Heaven or Hell.

Every love story has an ending, and ours ended abruptly. I was willing to wait for him to sort out his relationship and then come to me when he was ready. He even *asked* me to wait for him more than once. He told me it might take a few years for him to figure out his issues, but he wanted me to be patient. However, in the last conversation we ever had, he told me not to wait anymore. He wanted to work things out with his wife, so he said goodbye to me forever.

Although this happened many years ago, it still affects me to this day. I hear about couples who cheat on each other, break up, and then end up with the people they cheated with. Why didn't that happen to me? And why didn't I meet him sooner, before he got married? Was I *that* unlucky in love?

My takeaway: I was meant to meet Jeremy. Perhaps I was there to guide him back to his wife, and he was there to teach me about true love. I knew, with all my heart, that what I did was wrong, yet I couldn't stop myself from committing this sin. Having a physical or even emotional affair with a married man is absolutely wrong. I tried to make excuses for my actions, but I can only blame myself for being a part of such a despicable, forbidden relationship.

HOW MUCH DOES THAT BAGGAGE WEIGH?

Nate's online profile didn't say much about him, but I was interested to learn more. I felt a connection on our first date, and he asked me right away if I had kids or had ever been married. Those are common first date questions, especially once you get into your late 30s. As soon as I tell guys that the answer is no to both questions, the follow-up question is almost always, "What's wrong with you, then?" I've accepted that guys assume I have issues as an older single woman, but that's the way it goes.

After answering Nate's questions, I then asked him the same things. I was surprised to find out that he had two kids and was separated from his wife. I immediately tensed up. I didn't want to be on a date with a married man! He said the divorce papers were on the way, and he hadn't lived with her for three years. He promised me that it was indeed over between them.

After talking to him more, I discovered that he had just broken up with another woman a few days prior to our date. He admitted that she was in love with him, but he wasn't ready to be in a committed relationship with her. Everything he told me should've added up to enough red flags to say goodbye, but instead, I stupidly continued to date him.

I wanted things to work out between us, and I started seeing him almost daily. We had lots of similar interests and personality traits, but all of his baggage kept getting in the way. Whenever we were having a deep discussion, his kids would call him and interrupt. I couldn't let him ignore his kids, and he put them before me anyway. His soon-to-be ex-wife called all the time to talk about behavioral issues with the kids, so he had that to deal with as well. On top of that, the woman he had just broken up with was stalking him and begging to take her back. I was legitimately concerned for my safety once she learned of my existence.

I was way too tolerant of all the crap I dealt with when it came to Nate. I liked him so much that I didn't see the situation clearly. I wasn't courageous enough to end it, either. He had to be the one to cut things off. He had a lot of stuff to deal with, and dating me wasn't something he could add to his mess.

My takeaway: Don't date a guy who's newly separated, not ready for a committed relationship, or has too much on his plate. If the guy can't get through one date without pouring out his problems to you, he's probably not ready to be in a relationship. Plus, guys rarely marry the women they meet while separated and not yet fully divorced. Instead, you'll be a shoulder to cry on, the one who relieves his sexual tension, and the punching bag for the grief his ex is giving him.

OH, BROTHER!

I was dating Ben for a few months, and he never wanted to commit to a relationship with me. We enjoyed each other's company, but he didn't feel ready to settle down, at least not with me. His brother Ryan hung out with us one weekend, and I found myself getting a crush on Ryan.

Since my time dating Ben was coming to an end, I saw no problem in pursuing his brother. I knew it was messy and complicated, "keeping it in the family," but it felt like the right path for me. At the time, they seemed to be complete opposites, but, in retrospect, they still had the same core values and similarities that only brothers have.

When I started dating Ryan, I informed Ben of my decision. If I had asked for permission, Ben wouldn't have given it to me. As the saying goes, "It's better to beg for forgiveness than to ask for permission." I didn't feel that it was necessary to get approval from him. He made it clear that he didn't want to date me, so why not move on to his brother?

I knew my relationship with Ben would be shattered as soon as I started dating Ryan, but I didn't care. In my mind, Ben had hurt me beyond repair, and I was relieved to move on from him. I didn't expect to fall for his brother, but it felt like destiny to me. I wasn't trying to get revenge on Ben for breaking my heart. I honestly felt like I was meant to meet Ben so he could lead me to Ryan.

I put lots of effort into my relationship with Ryan because I wanted it to work so badly. I also knew how important the sibling bond should be, so I urged them to connect with each other more. I did not want to be the reason their brotherly relationship fell apart.

My romance with Ryan ended after a few months. One day he told me that he didn't want to date me anymore. He didn't give a reason, but I suspected that he felt guilty for hurting his brother. I was left in the dust after pouring so much of myself into our relationship. He got another girlfriend days after we broke up, and I heard from the grapevine that Ben was also happily dating someone new.

My takeaway: Dating brothers is not smart. Although I didn't date them simultaneously, it was still stupid of me.

SUMMARY

Do not date or pursue guys that are married, engaged, related to someone else you dated, or in a committed relationship. None of these relationships will end well for you. Ex-boyfriends may be tempting to date again, but keep in mind why you broke up. If a guy has too much baggage from past relationships, think hard before getting involved in his chaotic life.

CHAPTER 11

WHY DOES IT BURN WHEN I PEE?

Did you know that it takes three months for certain STDs to show up in a test? Every STD has a different incubation period. Many people never get tested or only do when they find out they've been exposed. I've always been cautious and get tested regularly, which is, unfortunately, not the norm.

PRANK CALLING GETS THE JOB DONE

I dated a guy who had lots of unprotected sex before me and even admitted that he had sex with a prostitute once. He never got tested, although I frequently urged him to make an appointment. After months of begging him to go to a free clinic with no action on his end, I finally decided to give him the push he needed.

I had my friend call him and pretend she was from Planned Parenthood. She said his ex-girlfriend had tested positive for gonorrhea, so he needed to come in and get tested. My plan worked! He made an appointment for the next day. Since my friend's call was a prank, it wasn't a real appointment, but at least it scared him enough to agree to get tested for everything.

He didn't talk to me for a full week after learning that I pranked him, but it pushed him to get a real test. His results came back negative for all STDs, and then I enjoyed my time with him without worrying about sexual diseases or infections.

THE INCUBATION PERIOD IS REAL!

I was dating Brett, whom I knew to be promiscuous. He slept around and begged to have sex with me from day one. I don't have sex on the first date, and when I do consent to sex, I want us to be exclusive. Brett was stubborn and didn't want to change his ways, but he seemed to like me enough to make an exception.

He put up a fight when I asked him to get tested, but he agreed only if I paid for his test. I told him that there were lots of free clinics around, but he would only go to his trusted doctor, who charged $100 for an STD panel. I grudgingly paid him and also reminded him that he had to abstain from sex for a few weeks before the test. I said he'd ideally have to wait three months to make sure he's past the incubation period, but we compromised on three weeks.

Brett's STD panel came back all negative, so then we started having daily sex. He was in touch with his sensations, and soon after, he began to complain about his body feeling off-kilter. He was in amazing shape and ate healthy food, but he constantly talked about something not feeling right.

He went back to his doctor and got a round of tests done to figure out what was wrong. The doctor smartly included STDs in the test, and, although he had just been tested a few weeks prior, the test came back positive for chlamydia. He admitted that he had unprotected sex the night before his first test, and he didn't think it would matter because he had been hooking up with her on and off for months.

I was furious that he ignored my request to abstain from sex for a few weeks. I was also concerned that I had contracted chlamydia. I hastily went and got tested. It came back negative, but I got tested every month for the next four months to be sure. I didn't touch a guy for those months in case I had it and was asymptomatic. I didn't want to spread it around because I actually care about the well-being of others! My relationship with Brett ended with his phone call about having chlamydia, and now I'm much more careful regarding my sexual partners.

PENIS FAILURES

Besides STDs, there are plenty of other issues that could create a problem in your sexual relationship.

COMMON REASONS FOR SEXUAL DYSFUNCTION

1. **Medication/prescription drugs:** Antidepressants, anti-anxiety drugs, blood pressure drugs, birth control pills, antihistamines, and herbal supplements can affect your libido.

2. **Disease:** Diabetes, arthritis, cancer, and heart disease can lower your sex drive.

3. **Menopause:** 40% of women have a loss of libido during this time.

4. **Low testosterone:** This declines as you age, so you may have less desire for sex as you get older.

5. **Stress/anxiety/depression:** These can all reduce your libido, whether you take medication for it or not.

6. **Sleep apnea:** This causes fatigue, which can lower your libido.

7. **Sexual ignorance/inexperience:** A lack of knowledge or experience can affect your sex drive.

8. **Traumatic sexual experiences:** If you were traumatized by an awful experience, it could affect your libido.

9. **Drugs/alcohol:** Alcohol is a depressant, which lowers your sex drive.

10. **Relationship issues:** If you often fight or lose attraction for your partner, you may not enjoy being intimate anymore.

If your relationship is thriving, but there's a sexual problem, then you should make an appointment with a doctor or therapist to figure out what's wrong. You may subconsciously know and not want to face the truth, but it will come back to haunt you when you want to be intimate with your partner.

HOUSTON, WE HAVE A PROBLEM

Tom was eager to please me, and he wanted me all to himself. When he kissed me, he pushed his face hard onto my lips, as if he wanted his face to meld into mine. As soon as we started dating, he got possessive and jealous of any guy who even looked at me. He got in a fistfight with a friend of his for commenting on my butt. We went to clubs, and he shoved any guy who brushed past me.

One time, we went to a bar, and while he was in the bathroom, a stranger came up and flirted with me. I was aware of Tom's jealousy, so I kept glancing toward the bathroom to make sure he didn't see my interactions with this stranger. A few minutes later, I watched the security guard drag Tom out of the bar. I ran out after him and discovered that he punched through the bathroom wall after seeing me talk to that other guy.

As scary as he was, I was hoping he'd turn that jealousy into passionate lovemaking! Unfortunately, whenever we tried, he couldn't stay hard. He had a different excuse every time—he was tired, he wasn't in the mood, or he had spent all day masturbating and was worn out. A few times, I surprised him at his place and thought that would excite him, but instead, he got angry that I showed up unannounced and blamed me for his soft penis.

He got a Viagra prescription and started taking that before our dates. This allowed him to stay hard, but it numbed all of his sensations and prevented him from feeling any pleasure. This sexual issue got in the way of our relationship. I tried to be patient with him, but he refused to face his issues. He blamed me more and more, and we bickered all the time. We finally stopped dating because his erectile dysfunction was too much of a problem for me to handle.

My takeaway: Because of Tom's possessiveness, jealousy, and anger, he clearly had mental health and emotional issues that he needed to work out. I urged him to seek counseling, but it was ultimately up to him to *want* to get help. I may be a sex coach, but helping someone I'm romantically involved with is unethical. I tried showing him books that could give him guidance, but he was stubborn and refused to take responsibility for his boner problems.

SUMMARY

Getting tested for STDs is a necessary part of dating. You should get checked out regularly for your health, and make sure the guy gets tested, too. If one of you has sexual issues that affect the relationship, the problem won't miraculously go away on its own. You need to get to the root of the problem and take care of it by seeing a specialist or talking to someone who can help you.

CHAPTER 12
LOSING SIGHT OF YOURSELF

I dated a bunch of guys in my 20s and even some in my 30s who wanted me to change who I am. They put me on a pedestal and thought I was an ideal partner for them, yet they wanted to form me into their perfect partner by changing the essence of me. They all liked how I appeared to be, but once they got to know me and learned that I was all wrong for them, they wouldn't rest until they tried to adjust my personality.

It's one thing to get plastic surgery and change a person's outside appearance, but you can't change a personality. My mom told me that my personality was apparent from birth. She got a sense of what I was like from the beginning. As much as people try to extinguish my flame, my fiery energy continues to shine through.

REAL / FAKE / REAL / FAKE

I dated a guy who seemed to enjoy my true personality. He urged me to be myself when it was just the two of us hanging out. Whenever we went out in public, though, he tried to force me to be a muted version of myself. And then, when it was just us again, he urged me to be my real self. I got frustrated jumping back and forth from my real personality to my fake one, and so I ended it with him to go back to being me 100% of the time.

ROAD RAGE IS NOT KID-FRIENDLY

One guy wanted me to change my beliefs about raising kids. We had only been dating for two weeks, and he was already talking in detail about how to discipline our future children. I could tell that we weren't an optimal match at that point, but I kept dating him in case things between us improved.

I was driving one day and yelled out, "Fuck!" when someone cut me off. He said, "Are you going to use that language in front of our kids?" I looked at him with disgust and almost said, "Get the fuck out of my car." Instead, I just scoffed at him and didn't speak the rest of the drive. When we got back to my apartment, he said he wanted to go to couples counseling. If you're clashing with someone after two weeks, you don't seek counseling. You break up! And that's exactly what I did.

YOU WON'T PUT OUT MY FIRE

I also dated a guy who tried to slowly change me, without either of us being aware of it at the time. We dated for two years, which is a large chunk of time to be with someone. He was sweet and kind. Not that I was the opposite, but I still had to adjust my demeanor to be more in line with his. I somehow became the sweet and kind woman he wanted me to be.

Close friends commented that I was different, and they couldn't pinpoint precisely what had changed about me. One friend said I was more mature and refined, which did not sound like a compliment to me! When we broke up, my real personality finally began to shine through again. My spark was back, and I vowed to never let it get blown out again.

IT'S CALLED ACTING BECAUSE IT'S NOT REAL

I was starring in a play with a guy, and he asked me out after the first week of rehearsals. My character in the play was shy, innocent, and naive, all qualities that I am not. As a decent actress, I was able to portray the character well, and the guy figured that's how I was in real life. He was shocked to learn how different my real personality was, and he urged me to be more like my character. He wanted to date the character, not me. He soon began to resent the real me, and we had to work extra hard to fool the audience into believing we were a happily married couple.

SUMMARY

Don't ever let a guy change who you are. If you find yourself changing your personality to be the version the guy wants you to be, you may lose sight of yourself.

CHAPTER 13

HELLO! IS THERE ANYBODY IN THERE?

46.4% of American adults experience some type of mental illness in their lifetime. Life brings about all sorts of traumatic experiences and events, so if you're looking for a guy with absolutely no baggage, that's nearly impossible to find. Any person who has lived a full life has experienced some sort of mental or emotional turmoil. The trick is to find a guy who is aware of it and getting the help he needs.

You have your own pile of issues to take care of, which could include mental illness, addiction, or trauma from your past. Dating a guy who's either not aware of his problems or not willing to get help from a professional is dangerous for the health of your relationship. You shouldn't sacrifice your own well-being and become his pseudo-therapist.

If the guy you're dating is emotionally unavailable due to mental illness or addiction, you need to stop dating him before he pulls you down with him. If he admits that he has a problem and wants to resolve his issues, then you can give him a chance to heal himself. However, you should give him time and space to get better on his own before you try dating him again.

CAN YOU FIX A BROKEN PERSON?

Kevin had an overly difficult upbringing. Both of his parents had passed away, and in addition to working hard to make ends meet, he was helping his sister raise three kids after her husband left her. His mom taught him how to be a fantastic and compassionate gentleman, and he was intelligent, witty, and generous.

He swept me off my feet, and I felt like I was in a fairy-tale romance with Kevin from the start. He opened up to me about his past, and we shared all our secrets with each other. I could sense sadness beneath his layer of humor and sarcasm, but I figured my positive outlook would melt away his unhappiness.

Once I got to know Kevin more, I realized that he couldn't shake his depression. No matter how uplifting I tried to be, I couldn't improve his mental state. I didn't have much experience with clinical depression, but I had a feeling that it was beyond the scope of my knowledge.

I wanted so badly to help him because I genuinely cared about him and knew there was an exceptional person underneath all his pain. I urged him to seek counseling, but he never did. Near the end of our time together, he wasn't fully present. It seemed like I was spending time with the ghost of Kevin. I felt horrible ending our relationship, but since he wasn't willing to get the help he needed, I didn't know what else to do.

My takeaway: It's not my job to "fix" a guy. If he has mental or emotional issues that he needs to work out, he should talk to a therapist. I often become the pseudo-therapist when I'm dating someone because my instinct is to help him. Even if I were a licensed psychologist, it's not appropriate to counsel a guy I'm dating. I saw signs of depression in Kevin after a few dates, but I ignored them. I didn't know how serious it was until I had already fallen for him. Now I know that if a guy has deep-rooted psychological issues, I won't date him unless he's willing to seek therapy.

DO YOU LIKE PIÑA COLADAS?

When Greg met me at a bar for our first date, he asked me what I wanted to drink. I told him I'm not much of a drinker, so I ordered a virgin piña colada (one of my favorite non-alcoholic drinks). He stared at me with a look of horror for a few seconds and then asked me how I can survive a first date without a few drinks. I filed that question away for later analysis and told him that I don't need alcohol to have a good time.

While I slowly sipped my virgin piña colada, Greg downed five alcoholic drinks. He soon forgot that he was the only one drinking, and he relaxed and opened up to me about his life. He was entertaining, charming, and hilarious. We left the bar and went for a walk to pass the time until he was sober enough to drive home.

For our second date, we went mini-golfing. It was a family place with lots of kids around, and Greg thought it would be more fun if he were a little tipsy. He pulled out a flask and took a few chugs before the first hole. He offered it to me, but I declined.

I soon discovered a pattern. Greg wanted to get drunk for all our dates. He was smart and handsome, so I was hoping that he was just nervous in the beginning stages of dating and thought alcohol was a sufficient way to relax. I subtly asked him about his drinking habits a few times, and he always laughed it off and said he drank a normal amount in social situations. He most likely had an extremely high tolerance because he drank so much and didn't ever appear drunk. The only change I noticed was that he perked up and got more energy after drinking.

Greg and I continued to date, and I kept coming up with unique date ideas that didn't involve drinking. However, he always had a flask with him or knew of a nearby bar where he could grab a quick drink. I invited him over for dinner one night, and as soon as he walked in, he asked for a drink. I rarely keep any type of alcohol in my apartment, so all I could offer him was water or juice. He declined, and we ate our dinner in silence.

After eating, I tried hard to make conversation with him. I wanted him to be as captivating as he had been on our other dates, but then it dawned on me: Greg was *boring*. His fun side came out when he was drinking, but otherwise, he didn't have much of a personality! Or, if he did, it was destroyed by years of alcohol abuse. I didn't feel a connection with Greg that night, and we both could tell that it was our last night together.

My takeaway: I knew Greg was an alcoholic, and I tried to change that part of him. He was beyond any help I could've given. He either didn't accept his alcoholism or didn't believe it was a serious issue. As long as he wasn't willing to admit it to himself, he wasn't a good match for me.

My European mystery man

I took a two-week trip to Europe with a group of young professionals. We all met a week before our flight to get to know each other. I was instantly attracted to Derek. He was tall, handsome, and mysterious. He seemed shy, but my outgoing personality got him to open up a little bit. I knew he was going to be my crush throughout that trip.

When we arrived at the airport, I went straight to him and talked about how excited I was for our trip. He was responsive but distant, and I couldn't figure out why. After going to the bathroom on the airplane, he came back smelling like cigarettes. Even though smoking on the plane was illegal, he said he had to get a few puffs in during our long flight. As a non-smoker, I was grossed out and disappointed, but I was still determined to date Derek, no matter what.

On our first night out in Europe, everyone ordered a drink or two, but I noticed that Derek didn't drink at all. He took me aside and admitted that he was in Narcotics Anonymous

(NA). He said he never had a problem with alcohol, but he used to smoke a lot of marijuana, and that turned into harder drugs, like meth, cocaine, and heroin. He became addicted, went to rehab, and relapsed. His parents sent him to jail to teach him a lesson, and he promised to go to NA meetings from then on.

As someone with no drug experience, everything he told me was fascinating. I thought I would be an ideal match for him because I was anti-drugs and figured I could help keep him on the right path. I was impressed that he seemed so stable, despite his many years of struggle.

My interest in Derek never waned, but I couldn't figure him out. He seemed into me one moment, and the next moment he didn't want to talk to me. It was strange behavior, but I liked him so much that I ignored all the signs that he wasn't ready to date. Whenever he acted distant, it made me want him even more.

Derek and I never discussed if we'd date when we got back to Los Angeles, but in my mind, we were already dating. Two weeks of creating memories on another continent meant something to me. After getting home, I started planning date ideas for the two of us, but Derek sadly disappeared after that trip. I reached out to him multiple times, but he never responded.

Months later, Derek sent me a long, heartfelt phone message saying he relapsed after the trip and knew it wasn't the right time for him to date. He got to the step in his recovery program about making amends, and he apologized for his behavior.

My takeaway: I ignored clear signs that Derek wasn't ready to date and tried to force a relationship anyway. Instead of enjoying my trip to Europe, I put all my energy into making it work with Derek. Now I know that if a guy is in recovery, he needs time to heal on his own before starting a relationship.

Summary

Do not date a guy who is emotionally unavailable due to mental illness or addiction. If you notice signs that he's unstable and not ready to date, then you should end it before getting sucked into his downward spiral. Admitting he has a problem is a good first step for him, but you should move on or at least give him time and space to get better before dating him.

CHAPTER 14
EW, WHAT'S THAT SMELL?

You walk into a room and lock eyes with the most gorgeous man you've ever seen. He miraculously comes up to you, but as soon as he introduces himself, you recoil at the sound of his voice. Why was such a handsome man given the voice of Daffy Duck? You politely excuse yourself and move on.

You find another equally gorgeous guy and decide to approach him to see if his voice sounds like Tweety Bird. Thankfully, this guy has a deep, sexy voice that draws you closer, but as soon as you step within a foot of him, you smell a strong scent that undeniably turns you off. It's not his cologne or aftershave. It's *his* scent. You pretend to wave to a friend and walk away.

Pay attention to your five senses when dating someone new.

SIGHT

Most people decide if they're attracted to someone within the first 90 seconds of meeting. You should be at least a little bit physically attracted to him in the beginning. That attraction can grow immensely, and maybe you will love other qualities he has that make up for his average looks. However, if he starts appearing unattractive to you over time, it's a sign that the relationship isn't meant to be.

I boldly asked out a guy after having a back-and-forth banter with him all night at a friend's dinner party. He was smart and funny, but I didn't find him physically attractive *at all*. We dated for a few weeks, but I could never get past his looks. Supposedly, attraction grows over time, but I couldn't find one redeeming quality about his appearance. I was surprised to learn that he got married soon after we dated, and his wife was stunning. Just goes to show that beauty is undoubtedly in the eye of the beholder!

SOUND

A man's voice can be pleasing to your ears, or it can sound like fingernails scratching on a chalkboard. If you enjoy his voice or are able to tolerate it, that's great! But if his voice makes you shiver with disgust, do you honestly want to put up with that sound for the rest of your life? The personality of the guy comes through when he speaks, too. Listen for tone, clarity, speed, and volume. Some of those qualities can change based on mood, but you'll still hear the essence of his voice and decide if it's attractive to you.

I was invited to an open mic night by a friend who wanted to set me up with one of the performers. About halfway through the show, she nudged me and pointed to the guy walking on stage. *That* was the guy she wanted to set me up with? I didn't find him attractive in the slightest. A few seconds later, he opened his mouth to sing, and the most beautiful sound came out of him. In a matter of seconds, I went from being unattracted to thinking he was the most gorgeous man on the planet. His voice made up for his subpar looks, and I was instantly hooked. A sexy speaking or singing voice can boost a guy's attraction by 1,000% for me!

SMELL

All your senses are important, but smell may be the number one element of attraction. What you smell is a powerful indicator of how compatible you are with someone. Some colognes and perfumes supposedly contain human pheromones, but you can't bottle up a person's actual scent. I hate when men mask their scents with cologne or body spray. Then it will just take longer for me to find out if we're compatible. If your major histocompatibility complex (MHC) genes are either too similar or too different, you won't be attracted to the guy's smell. You can't fight science. The guy's genetic makeup is either compatible with yours, or it's not.

I've always had an extraordinary sense of smell. While dating a guy, I got used to his scent and only desired that. Although I was exposed to lots of different male pheromones at work and walking down the street, my brain ignored those smells and just focused on the scent of the guy I was dating. After we broke up, my nose started to pick up on all the pheromones in the environment. Just like a bloodhound can sniff out a scent trail, I can sniff out all the attractive men in my surrounding area. Some would say it's a curse, but I find it a blessing to be so in tune with my sense of smell.

TASTE

Your sense of smell and taste are closely linked, so when you kiss a guy, you're not only smelling his scent, but you can taste it as well. Of course, if he just ate onions or garlic, the taste of that will overpower any pheromones, but enjoying the taste of his saliva and sweat means you are genetically compatible. Embrace his taste! If you have an aversion to his taste, you should figure out if it's something he ate or if it's the way he always tastes, no matter what he ingests. Trust your taste buds. They will send a signal to your brain, so don't ignore the signs you receive.

I was dating a guy who had a mild scent, but whenever we kissed, I tasted metal. At first, I thought he was eating something that would cause that, but I kept tasting it day after day. I offered him my toothpaste, which didn't make a difference. I knew that there were some possible causes for him to have a metallic taste in his mouth, like medication or vitamins or something more serious. I decided to gently probe one day and find out the cause. As soon as I said I tasted metal, he clammed up. He was obviously aware and didn't want to discuss it. He grew distant, and we didn't date for much longer after that.

TOUCH

We all like to be touched. Some more than others. Luckily this is the one sense that can be altered based on your preference. If you start dating a guy whose touch is too rough, you can guide him to caress you more gently. However, if you are repulsed by his touch, even when you teach him how you like it, then he's probably not the guy for you.

I went on two dates with a guy who was decent-looking and engaging. He was shy and didn't make any moves to touch me until the end of the second date. All he did was lightly place his hand on the small of my back as we were walking. My whole body instantly tensed up. I froze, and I think my heart stopped beating for a few seconds. It felt like a heavy brick covered in fire and ice hit my back all of a sudden. I wanted to shout, "Get it off of me!" but instead, I just subtly pulled away. He sensed that touching me made me uncomfortable, so he took his hand away. He didn't do anything bad or aggressive, but just that simple touch caused such a negative reaction in my entire body. I knew he was not for me, and we never saw each other again.

SUMMARY

Your five senses are all important indicators of your attraction for a guy you're dating. Some of your senses might work better than others, but any sign you receive from your sense of sight, sound, smell, taste, or touch shouldn't be ignored.

PART THREE

CREATING A LIFE TOGETHER

CHAPTER 15

DO I FEEL BUTTERFLIES OR NAUSEA?

Did you know that if you second-guess yourself, you're more likely to make a worse decision than if you go with your first instinct? Your intuition knows what is right for you, and you should listen to that tiny voice in the back of your head.

Although the difference between feeling butterflies versus nausea is slight, following your instinct is important when it comes to dating. You might ignore your intuition because you feel incredible attraction for the guy, but you'll learn down the line that you should've trusted your gut all along.

When you have doubts about a guy, it's common to convince yourself that everything is fine. You suppress your feelings because you don't want to face reality. You continue with the relationship because it's comfortable and easy. **If you have an inkling that it's wrong, get the courage to end it**. You must listen to yourself. If you push your gut feeling aside, you'll face much bigger consequences later. Maybe not today. Maybe not tomorrow. But you'll eventually have to deal with the fact that your relationship isn't right for you.

IS IT JUST COLD FEET?

Becky said yes when her boyfriend proposed, but she had a sick feeling in the pit of her stomach about agreeing to marry him. She couldn't explain it, but her intuition was telling her not to do it. She pushed her doubts away and figured she was just having cold feet. The next few months went by in a whirlwind as she planned the wedding of her dreams and found a perfect house for them to move into as a married couple.

Becky confided in me a week after her big day. She told me that she brought up her feelings of unease with her family, but they all urged her to go through with it anyway. She admitted that she felt slightly sick the entire time she was planning her wedding, and she knew her gut was speaking to her and telling her to call off the wedding. She didn't trust her intuition, though, and she got married. They moved into the house she found for them, but she couldn't shake the feeling that he wasn't right for her.

She felt obligated to stay with him, but that sick feeling in her stomach never disappeared. Some nights she'd stay awake for hours wondering if she made the biggest mistake of her life marrying this guy. Their relationship slowly dissolved, and they ended up divorced a few years later.

My takeaway: You should always trust your gut. Many couples stay together much longer than they should because they feel guilty about ending it. Although I've never been married and divorced, I'm surely guilty of ignoring my intuition and staying with a guy, despite my feelings of unease. Ending a toxic relationship is a huge step, but it's the only option if you want to have a bright, fulfilling life.

CHEMISTRY IS A TRICKY THING

When you're into a guy, you'll feel butterflies, just like you'll feel nausea when a guy repulses you. Intuition and chemistry go hand in hand. Your intuition will tell you if you have chemistry with a guy. If you feel absolutely nothing for him, then that's a telltale sign that there is no chemistry.

A PICTURE-PERFECT DATE

I had a first date planned with a guy named Edward. I was excited because he looked sexy in his pictures, and I had just finished reading the *Twilight* books (the main character was Edward). I couldn't believe my luck when I walked into the restaurant and saw a guy just as gorgeous as I imagined.

To an outsider, our date seemed perfect. We told each other funny stories, opened up about our families, and shared a slice of cheesecake after a delicious meal. We had similar backgrounds and interests and goals for the future. It didn't hurt that he had a dazzling smile and was immaculately dressed. We spent three hours at the restaurant, and then he walked me to my car and gave me a quick, yet gentle kiss on the lips.

Sometimes I overanalyze my dates, but I didn't think about my date with Edward at all. A few days went by, and then a week went by, and I didn't hear from him. And the intriguing thing was that I didn't care. It was almost as if our date just slipped out of my memory. It wasn't until a few weeks later, when I was on my way out to see a new guy, that my roommate asked if I was still dating Edward.

And that's when it hit me. Edward and I had zero chemistry. Although our date was ideal and he checked all the boxes for what I wanted in a man, I felt nothing for him. He obviously felt the same way since I never heard from him again.

I ran into him at a movie premiere a few months later. We smiled at each other and cordially said, "Good to see you." Then we went our separate ways forever.

My takeaway: You can't force chemistry. It's either there, or it's not.

BUTTERFLIES CAN TURN INTO NAUSEA IF YOU'RE NOT CAREFUL

I was working as an event planner in Los Angeles. I had to drive to a park in the middle of nowhere for the day, and when I arrived, I realized that 20 different huge fields were all occupied with different events. I drove around in a panic, frantically looking for the right field. I felt a pull toward field #18, but I decided to stop at fields 1–17 first. When I pulled up in front of field #18, I just knew in my gut that it was the right place. There were few cars in that section, and there was no indication that anything was going on there. However, I parked my car and started walking toward the field. Way in the distance, I saw a figure, and I felt drawn to it.

I finally reached the figure, and it was Matt, my assistant for the day. We locked eyes, and a strange feeling washed over me. As a teenager, I was totally boy-crazy, and this felt like the adult version of that. I felt instant chemistry with this guy just from being in the same vicinity as him. He was cute, silly, and had a dark sense of humor that I related to.

We spent ten hours together setting up the event, running it, and cleaning up afterward. The hours flew by, and I enjoyed every second of my day with him. I didn't want to say goodbye, so I invited him to a party that night. He agreed, and we talked until the sun came up the next morning. The only problem was that he had a girlfriend. He said they were having issues, so I took that to mean they were about to break up.

We got top-notch reviews from that event, so my company kept pairing us together. I couldn't wait for the weekends because I knew I'd be spending both days with Matt. The summer eventually came to an end, and I knew I had to continue seeing him. He mentioned that he wanted to move to a new apartment, and, although my living situation was sufficient, I decided it was time for me to move, too—as long as it was with him!

I spent hours driving all over the city to find the optimal apartment, while he just passively waited and let me do all the hard work. I finally found a spacious, affordable apartment, so we moved in a few weeks later. While I was unpacking and organizing my room, Matt went to spend time with his girlfriend. I tried to secretly send negative energy toward their relationship, and, to my complete amazement, it worked! Matt burst through the door, collapsed on the floor, and cried to me about his breakup. Internally, I was thrilled, but I put on a solemn face and sympathized with him as he let out his feelings.

He opened a bottle of wine and swiftly downed the whole thing. I wanted to be considerate of his mourning process, but in his drunken stupor, he practically threw himself at me. I had been dreaming about being intimate with him from the second I laid eyes on him, but I didn't want it to be like this. He was drunk and sad and not thinking straight. I pushed him away and asked if he was sure he wanted to do this, and he said, "Yes, definitely." I pointed to the empty bottle of wine with raised eyebrows, and he said, "Don't worry, I'm not drunk at all." Yeah, right! (Side note: I later discovered that he could indeed hold his alcohol. I'd watch him drink many beers in a row and not show any signs of being drunk.) It was our first night alone together in our new apartment, and we had already broken the unwritten rule: Don't hook up with your roommates.

Whatever feelings I had for Matt quadrupled after having sex with him. I tried to separate those feelings, but I had such a strong attachment to him. We both found new jobs, and I rushed home every day after work to spend time with him. Once in a while, he was there, but he often went out with his friends and got home extremely late. If I was still awake, he'd come into my room to have sex with me. He was always vague about where he went or what he was doing. I was suspicious of his late-night escapades, but I ignored my misgivings and tried to enjoy my time with him whenever I got it.

Matt was immensely intuitive and seemed to always know what I was thinking. I'd be humming a tune in my mind, and Matt would oddly start singing it. Most of my thoughts were of him, so I became afraid to think at all while in my apartment! Because he was so in tune with my emotions, I thought that meant his feelings for me were as strong as mine were for him. Little did I know, he was out spilling his seed all over town while I curled up in bed, fantasizing about our future together.

A few months later, I was awoken by a creaking noise. Before I could place the sound, I heard a high-pitched moan, and a sick feeling washed over me. The wall separating our bedrooms was thin, and I heard every whisper, groan, and giggle that came out of them. After being secretive about his sexual encounters for months, Matt finally brought a girl home. He was smart and knew me well at that point, so I figured he brought her there as a warning to me—his passive-aggressive way of telling me he's not interested in me as a dating prospect. I got the message.

We never discussed the girl he brought home, but our relationship changed after that night. He never attempted to have sex with me again, and I never made any indication that I wanted it. He had my whole heart, and every time he came home late, a piece of my heart chipped off. The night he brought that girl over, my heart shattered. It took years for my heart to heal, and when I found out he had gotten married, I curled up in bed, just as I used to, and wept for hours.

My takeaway: Just because I felt intense chemistry with him, it didn't mean he felt the same. My intuition continually told me to stop pursuing him, but I ignored all the warning signs I got from my body. It was a huge mistake to live with a guy I was interested in dating. Our roommate relationship got in the way of any romantic relationship we could've had. He didn't have to take me out on real dates; instead, I was always available to him as a backup whenever he was in the mood for intimacy. The saying, "Why buy the cow when you can get the milk for free?" applied to our unhealthy relationship. If I had played "hard to get," perhaps there would've been a future for us.

SUMMARY

Always trust your intuition. Whether you feel butterflies, nausea, or nothing, pay attention to what your gut tells you. Also, you must understand that chemistry is sometimes not reciprocated. If your intuition is telling you that the guy doesn't feel the same way, you can't force him to want you.

CHAPTER 16
CROSS-COUNTRY MOVING IS THE BEST!

Y ou meet a guy while on vacation and undeniably hit it
off. You have unbelievable chemistry, your personalities
are in sync, and you feel connected to him on all levels.
The weekend ends, and you promise to keep in touch. You
live 1,000 miles apart, which isn't a deal-breaker but is also
not optimal for starting a relationship.

You talk to him regularly and grow attached to him, despite
the distance and inability to spend time with him in person.
He comments that it would be nice if you lived closer, and you
take that as permission to move to his city. You say goodbye
to your current life and impulsively drive across the country
to be with him.

Although the weekend you spent together was fabulous,
reality sets in as soon as you arrive. You agree that it's too
soon to move in with him, so you find your own place and
get a temporary job to hold you over until you find something
more stable. He introduces you to his friends, and you join
their social circle with ease.

Your relationship goes well for the first few months, but,
as it often happens, you grow apart and break up. The friends
you made are loyal to him, so you lose your social circle and
are stuck in a new city, not having any support system.

Moving for a guy may seem appealing, but it rarely ends well. If you're like me, you love to take big risks when it comes to love. My recommendation is to wait until you're absolutely sure you're going to end up with this guy before moving.

REASONS IT'S ACCEPTABLE TO MOVE FOR A GUY

1. You're engaged or married.

2. You've already lived near each other and dated exclusively for at least six months (ideally a year), and **he asks you to move for him.** You've discussed the future, and you plan on being with each other forever.

3. You live far apart, but you have spent a substantial amount of time together in person. You have dated exclusively for at least a year, and **he asks you to move to his city.** You've discussed the future, and you plan on being with each other forever.

There are always exceptions, but these are the guidelines I suggest. If a guy does not clearly ask you to move for him, it means he's not all in. When you're the one who suggests that you move to be with him, it changes the male-female dynamic, and your relationship is probably doomed.

If the guy asks to move to *your* city, the above reasons still apply. And please don't let him move for you unless you're sure you want to be with him long-term.

I WILL FOLLOW YOU ACROSS THE UNIVERSE

My friend Stephanie was living in Los Angeles. From my perspective, she had a superb life: a lucrative job, a gorgeous boyfriend, and a moderately priced apartment. Her world was turned upside down when her boyfriend, Luke, got a promotion and had to move to New York City. They had been seriously dating for a year, and he was whisked away by his company before she had time to mentally process his move.

Because everything happened so quickly, they didn't get a chance to have a real discussion about how they'd cope with a long-distance relationship. Luke didn't ask her to move to NYC to be with him, but she was doubtful that they'd survive as a couple being so far apart. She did what any woman in love would do. She quit her job, broke her apartment lease, and booked a one-way ticket to NYC.

I supported her decision, but I feared that it would all blow up in her face eventually. It happened much sooner than I expected. Stephanie told me that Luke seemed weirded out that she gave up her amazing life in LA to be with him. They spent all their free time together, but they started fighting about tiny issues that never used to be a problem.

Luke finally admitted that he felt weighed down by her presence. He wanted to explore the city as a single man. Stephanie said she resented him for moving without taking their relationship into account. They broke up, and Stephanie had to start from scratch, building a life for herself in NYC.

IS MOVING DURING A SNOWSTORM A BAD OMEN?

I was living in Portland and hanging out with some friends when I met a cute guy named Brandon. He was visiting from Los Angeles for the weekend, and I was delighted to discuss a city I had lived in and missed. We totally hit it off and spent the rest of the weekend together. We exchanged numbers, but I tried to put him out of my mind.

To my surprise, Brandon called me the second he landed at LAX. It almost felt like he had never left. We were soon in constant contact. First texting, and then exchanging late-night phone calls, and finally, daily Skype calls. In fact, we jumped onto Skype multiple times a day, if possible, and I hated when I had plans and had to stop communicating with Brandon for even an hour.

I visited Brandon twice, and it was clear that our relationship was progressing. I didn't want to have a long-distance relationship for too long, so I made the spontaneous decision to move back to LA to be with him. Everyone I talked to said it was a dreadful idea, especially since we had only known each other for three months. Did I want to pick up and move back to the place I left?

I ignored everyone's advice and moved in with Brandon. He was applying for grad school, and I urged him to apply all over the country. I thought it would be a good idea for us to have a fresh start in a new city as a couple. A few months later, we drove across the country to Maryland, and since I was so eager to make the move and start our new life as soon as possible, we drove in the dead of winter. We hit multiple snowstorms on our way and even arrived in Maryland as the city was shutting down due to a huge storm.

We settled into a cozy apartment, and the euphoria of our new life together in a new city speedily wore off. I started to see Brandon clearly for the first time in our relationship. I realized that we weren't compatible at all! I felt that I had to make it work, though, because I moved twice for this guy. It just *had* to work.

Brandon was smart, and he could tell that things were off between us, too. After his first week of classes, he came home and broke up with me. Although I knew way down deep in my heart that our breakup was necessary, I was still devastated. I wasn't able to afford the apartment on my own, so I moved out and found a new place to live. My supervisor at work noticed that I wasn't my cheerful self, so I got fired a few days later. I had to start over on my own. I had no friends, no job, and an aching heart to deal with.

My takeaway: I look back on that time with such disappointment in my decisions. I moved twice for a guy I barely knew. Not even to a new zip code, but to two different states. One of them across the entire country! The first move was after talking to him for just three months. That's not long enough to fully know someone. I got carried away with the thrill of it all, and I made awful choices along the way. Moving in with him right away was also stupid of me, but it made the most sense logistically. I knew we wouldn't stay in LA that long, and I didn't even consider the possibility of us breaking up when we searched for a place to live in Maryland.

Summary

Do not move for a guy unless you're sure it's going to last with him. This means you're already married or engaged, or you've discussed a future with him and agree that you'll be together forever. I don't discourage taking risks for love, but it's important to learn as much as possible about each other and confirm that he's "the one" before making that big move.

CHAPTER 17

I'M NOT GETTING ANY YOUNGER...

Guys seem to have all the time in the world to settle down and get married. Unfortunately, women have a ticking clock. We're not going to have a million eggs in our body forever, so we can't keep waiting for guys to be ready for a commitment. Even if having kids is not a priority, it would be nice if men were on the same timeline as us.

I have waited for guys in all stages of the dating process, short term and long term.

EXAMPLES OF WHAT I'VE WAITED FOR

1. Waited for the guy to text or call

2. Waited for the guy to ask me out

3. Waited for the guy to show up on the date

4. Waited for the guy to want to date exclusively

5. Waited for the guy to ask to be my boyfriend

6. Waited for the guy to introduce me to his friends

7. Waited for the guy to introduce me to his family

I've also heard tons of excuses for why the guy is not ready to take it to the next phase (meaning engagement or marriage).

Reasons I've continued waiting

1. He wants to finish school

2. He wants to get a promotion

3. He wants to have more savings

4. He wants to wait until he's a certain age

5. He wants to wait until his older sibling gets married

6. He wants to wait a set amount of time

7. He wants to be unquestionably sure of his decision

In all of these circumstances, I have been the fool who continues waiting—and waiting—and waiting with no ending date in sight. Often, when the guy does finally accomplish his goal, he comes up with another excuse to make me wait all over again.

Will I wait until I'm old and gray?

I waited two years for a guy to finish graduate school. He promised to take our relationship to the next phase as soon as he graduated, but then he pushed that back until he got the job he desired. After he got his dream job, he said he wanted to wait until he was 35 before he considered marriage. And then his sister got engaged, and he didn't want to take the spotlight away from her. He wanted to wait until after her wedding before he proposed to me. I got a glimpse of my future—constantly waiting for something that would never happen. After waiting way too long, I finally ended it with him.

HOLLYWOOD IS WHERE DREAMS DIE

I was dating a brilliant, creative guy named Jared, who longed to be a famous screenwriter. His scripts were impressive, and he continually submitted his work to agents and writing contests with no luck. He promised me that we'd get engaged as soon as his first script was made into a movie.

As a new resident of Los Angeles, I figured that would happen in no time. However, months and months went by, and I recognized that it could take years, if not decades, for Jared's dream to become a reality. I wanted him to succeed, for his sake and mine, so I started promoting his scripts to everyone I met.

I was also longing to "make it" in Hollywood on the acting side, and getting rejected from auditions became a daily occurrence for me. I sometimes got a rejection letter six months after going to an audition, but that was better than waiting forever with no response.

While attending an acting class, the teacher told us something that stuck with me and made me give up my Hollywood dream of acting. His words were meant to be inspirational, but I got discouraged and lost all hope of succeeding in the acting world. He said that millions of people pursue acting, but only two percent make enough to earn a living. Those few that make it get by with hope, prayer, and a lot of waiting. Some catch their big break immediately, while the majority wait at least seven years until they're noticed. And then it takes another seven years to build their careers. He said if I'm patient enough to wait, whether it takes two years or thirty, I'll eventually be successful.

I walked out of that class feeling confident in my decision to give up the Hollywood dream. I also realized that I wasn't willing to wait at least seven years for Jared to be noticed. I promptly broke up with him and stopped dating guys in the entertainment industry who were waiting to be discovered.

My takeaway: Los Angeles is full of people waiting, but their dreams usually die with them. I got sucked into the waiting game, hoping and praying that I'd be the one to make it. I was drawn to Jared for pursuing his passion, but he, unfortunately, had no more luck than I did. It has been ten years, and Jared is still waiting for his big break. I'm glad I'm not by his side waiting with him.

SUMMARY

Don't put your life on hold and wait for a guy. He may come up with more excuses to push off the future that you want. If your goal is to get married, and he continuously makes you wait until he's ready, you could very well be waiting forever.

CHAPTER 18
OH, YOU ACTUALLY DON'T WANT KIDS?

You have a lovely chat with a guy before agreeing to meet, and you start to discuss deeper issues. He mentions that his last girlfriend dumped him because he wanted his own kids while she had two children from a previous marriage and didn't want more. You decided at a young age that you don't want kids, so you bring that up in the conversation. You both realize that you're not compatible, so you cancel your date and move on.

Before going on a first date, you should be clear of your relationship requirements. These are qualities that must be present for your relationship to work. They are non-negotiable, so if any quality is missing, you would have to eventually stop dating. You don't want to waste time with the wrong person, and the relationship *will* fall apart if you don't agree on one of those requirements.

It's necessary to bring these up early on in dating. If you wait too long, you could get attached to the guy and then find out your requirements won't be met.

THE MOST COMMON RELATIONSHIP REQUIREMENTS

1. **Wanting kids:** Be sure to have this discussion early on in dating. It's possible for people to change their minds, but you shouldn't assume that your partner will want them just because you do. Having a heart-to-heart about your wishes related to children is helpful for the growth of your relationship. You can learn a lot about each other and assess how strongly you both feel on this matter.

2. **Sex and intimacy:** It's not the only aspect of a relationship, but sex is important for the health of your partnership. Make sure you're in agreement with how sex plays a part in your lives. You should be able to talk openly about sexual issues and discuss how to handle different levels of desire.

3. **Fidelity:** Everyone has a different idea of what constitutes cheating. You may decide that any form of infidelity will not be tolerated, or perhaps you'll allow drunken kissing now and then. There's also emotional cheating, which some people think is innocent, and others feel is grounds for divorce. You could have an open marriage with a "don't ask, don't tell" policy or an open marriage where you tell each other everything.

4. **Financial responsibility:** Money is the most common reason for divorce, so discussing your financial situation upfront can help you be more open about other topics. It's an uncomfortable subject for many, but it's a necessary conversation to have if you want to spend your life together. If you like to save money for a vacation while he spends everything right away, you'll need to come up with a compromise. Planning

for your financial future can decrease conflicts about money later on.

OTHER RELATIONSHIP REQUIREMENTS THAT COULD BE IMPORTANT TO YOU

1. Similar life visions

2. Smoking/drugs/alcohol use

3. Wanting pets/animal involvement

4. Open communication

5. Level of education

6. Shared religious beliefs

7. Healthy mind/body/spirit

8. Mutual respect

9. Emotional intimacy

10. Time spent together/apart

After making your list, you can discover if the guy you're dating is a good match for you by seeing if he meets your requirements. You may change your mind about a requirement, and then it's important to let the guy know before it's too late.

FIRST COMES LOVE, THEN COMES MARRIAGE, THEN COMES...

Kate didn't think she wanted kids. She met a guy named Alex, and they dated for a while and fell in love. He was relieved that she didn't want kids because he didn't want the hassle of children either.

After being together for three years, Kate's feelings about wanting kids started to change. She watched how sensational he was with his nephew, and she longed to bring a baby into the world and pass on both of their traits to another person. Kate figured that Alex had changed his mind too, but they never discussed it. Alex proposed, and Kate joyfully said yes. They got so caught up in planning their wedding that Kate forgot to mention how she changed her mind about wanting kids.

Fast forward two years. Kate and Alex settled into their routine of married life, and they went to visit Alex's nephew one weekend. As they sat on the couch watching the little boy play with his blocks, Kate looked at Alex and whispered, "How about we start trying now?" Alex looked at her in horror and said, "What? I thought we agreed that we're not having kids!" The color drained from Kate's face as she came to the realization that they would never agree on this topic.

They had a blowout argument later that night, and they spent the next ten months fighting about whether they should have kids or not. Kate recognized that she could have gone through the whole process of pregnancy and labor during this time, but instead, she was stuck having the same argument over and over again.

They got divorced a few months later, and Kate looked back on the last six years of her life with sorrow. She was in her late thirties and had to start her search again. She was finally clear on her desire to have children and made this known to anyone she dated.

My takeaway: Having kids is a major decision, and lots of people change their minds as they get older. Kate decided she wanted kids before she got married and would've saved herself years of heartache had she admitted this to Alex. If you're unsure about wanting kids, make sure you gain clarity before dating someone.

A FRIENDLY TRIP TO THE MOVIE THEATER

I was dating Kyle for a few months, and we both loved movies. We saw numerous movies together at the theater and at home, and I was always interested in discovering what he'd suggest we watch next. I had a male friend named Phil, who also loved movies, and before Kyle and I started dating, I'd frequently see movies with Phil.

One day, Phil called and asked if I was free to catch a movie. I didn't have plans with Kyle that day, so I agreed. We got a quick dinner, watched the movie, and then went out for drinks afterward. It was completely casual, and Phil knew I was dating someone else. I went home and called Kyle to tell him about my evening. Kyle listened to me and then said he was tired and hung up.

As I was getting ready for bed, I heard pounding on my door. I looked through the peephole and saw Kyle standing there, red-faced and angry. I let him in, and he went off on a rant about how my actions were inappropriate and disrespectful to him. He claimed that I cheated on him by seeing a movie with another guy.

This turned into a terrible fight between us, and we never came to an agreement. To Kyle, seeing a movie with another guy constituted cheating, while I thought having sex with another guy was the only thing that counted as cheating. We had never discussed our interpretations of fidelity, and we both paid the price for our different beliefs on the topic.

For the sake of our relationship, I never spent time with Phil or any other male friends again while dating Kyle. I didn't agree with his reasoning, but I wanted to respect his wishes.

My takeaway: I assumed that we were on the same page about fidelity, but I didn't realize how different his beliefs would be from mine. Now, I'll ask a guy what is allowed and what constitutes cheating. I don't want either of us to do anything that makes the other uncomfortable.

I know some couples who agree to not spend any alone time with a person of the opposite sex, excluding family. As I've matured and experienced how easy it is to develop feelings for someone I'm not dating, I agree with them. When I had my fight with Kyle, I was young and stubborn. I didn't think it would be a problem. Now I know better. Men and women cannot just be friends. Even if you feel nothing for your male friend, you have no idea if he's attracted to you and wants to act on his feelings.

This is especially true if you remain friends with an ex. You were attracted to each other at some point, so it's not fair to your current partner if you spend time with an ex.

YOU CAN'T HAVE YOUR CAKE AND EAT IT TOO

Danielle and Patrick were in an open marriage. It was her idea, and although he believed in monogamy, he agreed to this arrangement to please his wife. They promised to be honest and open about their dating habits with each other and with the people they dated on the side.

Danielle was extremely outgoing and flirtatious with every man she met, while Patrick was introverted and shy. Danielle easily filled up her evenings with various dates, and Patrick mainly stayed home, sulking about their arrangement. He was afraid that if he told her having an open marriage was a deal-breaker, she'd leave him.

Danielle continued having fun with other men and urged her husband to put himself out there and date a few women. Patrick finally did go on a date, and he was surprised by how much he enjoyed it. He felt drawn to this other woman, and he began to see her regularly. One of their open marriage rules was to not fall in love with anyone else, but Patrick couldn't help it. He fell hard and fast, and he eventually left Danielle for this other woman.

My takeaway: Open marriages usually end in disaster. There are exceptions, like if both people are 100% on board and willing to make enough time for each other. However, if one person isn't accepting of the arrangement, it will fail. If Danielle had told Patrick of her interest in having an open marriage early on in their dating, they wouldn't have wasted each other's time and gone through a messy divorce.

HONESTY IN YOUR DATING PROFILE

Another important relationship requirement is honesty. I am always honest, and I value honesty in my relationships. When I catch a guy I'm dating in a lie, I instantly lose respect for him and end the relationship.

Many guys lie about how old they are, especially if you find them on a dating site. They don't reveal their last name, so you can't look them up to find out the truth. I've been on plenty of dates where I showed up, and the guy looked like he was my dad's age. It was still the same guy from the profile picture, but he had aged about 30 years. It's uncomfortable for both of us. He knows he lied, I know he lied, and we both know there won't be a second date.

I always call them out on it and question them, but they're evasive about it. I've never walked out on a date for lying about his age in his profile, but it's not a pleasant experience. If you're able to get the guy's last name before you meet, then you can look him up on Facebook or do an online search to find out his age. Sometimes it takes a little digging, but it's worth it!

A LITTLE WHITE LIE MAKES ALL THE DIFFERENCE

Marcus was a great catch. He was handsome, successful, and intelligent. I wanted to date him myself, but he wasn't interested in me. He told me that he lied about his age by one year on his dating profile (he wrote that he was 39 instead of 40) because he felt like there was a stigma for 40-year-old single men. Marcus dated a woman for a few months, but then his birthday rolled around, and he admitted that he was turning 41. She dumped him on the spot. I don't think she was bothered by his age, but the fact that he lied was a deal-breaker for her.

It's not worth it to lie. The truth will come out, so why stall the inevitable? You may meet a terrific guy who doesn't consider honesty a relationship requirement, but then you might worry that he's constantly lying.

SUMMARY

Figure out your relationship requirements and learn your date's relationship requirements to decide if you're compatible.

CHAPTER 19
THE VACATION TEST

You've probably heard that the way a man treats his waiter is telling of his personality. I find that statement to be 100% accurate. I've been on dates where the men are condescending, demanding, or just plain rude to the waiter. Even if they hold back from being that way around me, they eventually show their true nature and treat me the same way. On the other hand, when men are friendly and generous with the waiter, it's a good sign that they'll be that way with me in the long run.

When dating a guy, you get to experience his behaviors and personality changes in all sorts of environments and events.

WATCH HOW A GUY BEHAVES IN THESE CIRCUMSTANCES

1. When he's angry

2. When he's drunk

3. In an emergency

4. While on vacation

I had a friend who told me how she weeded out men on dates. She'd excuse herself at the restaurant and ask the waiter to "accidentally" spill water on her date to see how he'd react. If her date got angry and yelled at the waiter, she'd never go out with him again. If he laughed it off, she'd be hopeful that he was a potential future boyfriend.

As angry as the Hulk

Everyone has a unique way of showing anger. Some people clam up and lock themselves in their room until they calm down. Others lash out at anyone in their path. Some appear to be a ticking time bomb. Their anger is palpable in the air, and if you make the slightest movement or comment to set them off, they'll explode. There's no right or wrong way to be angry, but what matters is if you can accept the guy's way of being angry.

I dated a guy who always seemed to be angry. He was on edge about work, or an interaction with a friend, or a car that cut him off on the way over. No matter what situation we were in, he always had a reason to be angry. He was a constant ticking time bomb, and I was afraid to say anything that would bring out his rage. I couldn't tolerate his incessant anger, and so I broke up with him.

Are you a silly or sad drunk?

I've also realized that a guy's true colors show when he's drunk. Is he relaxed and calm? Or moody and emotional? Or angry and aggressive? You can be the judge of his drunk personality to see if it's something you're willing to tolerate. Of course, one drunken encounter may be different from another. If he had a bad day and wants to numb his feelings with alcohol, his mood will be different than a lighthearted night of drinking at a party.

ONLY REAL MEN CRY

I dated a guy who always cried when he drank. He knew this would be the outcome if he started drinking, but he seemed to look forward to that release of emotion. He was so focused on work during the week that he wanted to truly feel his emotions on the weekend. He drank a bottle of wine every Saturday and cried it all out. At first, it was flattering that he was willing to be so vulnerable and open with me, but I didn't enjoy his drunken crying after a few weeks. I ended it soon after.

NO NEGATIVITY ALLOWED IN MY ROOM!

If there's an emergency and you have to be rushed to the hospital, would you want your date around to keep you company? Emergencies can, unfortunately, happen at any time, and the way a guy behaves during significant life events is revealing of his personality. In a natural disaster, does he panic or take appropriate actions to resolve the situation? If you're injured, does he freak out or take charge and help you?

After hitting my head while on a date, I was taken to the emergency room to check for brain damage. I knew I was fine, but the doctor wouldn't let me move for eight hours until he had completed all the necessary testing. The guy I was dating was allowed to be in the room with me, and I didn't like his negative energy. He was probably just worried about me, but he kept pacing and mumbling to himself and making sarcastic comments about the situation. I appreciated the fact that he stayed by my side all day, but I could tell that he was not the type of person I'd want to go through life's ups and downs with.

A few months later, I had to get some emergency blood-work done, which always makes me uneasy. I asked a male friend to accompany me, and I was amazed by his calming effect. He was affectionate and caring throughout the whole ordeal, so all my nervousness melted away. His gentle presence and positivity got me through the day, and it brought us so much closer. We ended up dating for a few months because of how he acted during my emergency.

VACATION ADVENTURES

Going on vacation is always a blast. It's even better when you have a date to go with. An added bonus of going on vacation with a guy is that you get to see how he acts when he's out of his element. You're sharing new experiences together in a new environment, and you can't always control your surroundings. Does he plan out every minute of the trip or go with the flow and see where the wind takes you? Either method is fine as long as he's in sync with your method.

If you decide to go on a trip with a guy you're dating, you can pay attention to how he behaves in different circumstances:

1. **On the drive there:** Do you take turns driving? What's his driving personality? Does he have road rage or drive like he's 90 years old? Does he take a nap when it's your turn or keep you entertained with stories and car games? Do you compromise on types of music to listen to?

2. **On the flight:** If you take a plane to your destination, how does he treat you on the flight? Is he good company? Is he excited or nervous about flying? Does he leave you enough leg and arm space or take over both seats?

3. **At the hotel:** When you walk into your hotel room, this is probably the first time you're sharing a space that doesn't belong to either of you. Does he take over the whole room and unpack freely? Or does he divide the space equally to give you just as much space for your stuff? Does the room look like a

tornado went through it after one night in there? Or does it look untouched and sparkling clean?

4. **While exploring:** If this vacation consists of going to the beach and relaxing in the sun, then there isn't much planning needed for activities. However, if you're going on excursions and visiting places of interest, do you agree on how you're spending the day? Does he plan out all activities without checking with you? Or are you pleased to let him lead the trip?

5. **When problems arise:** You can't control the weather, so do you have backup plans if it's raining the whole time you're supposed to be outside? Does he get frustrated with changing or canceling plans? If there's an issue with your hotel room, does he get worked up or angry about switching rooms?

All of these are questions to consider when you're vacationing with a date. If he has one or two negative behaviors, it's not necessarily a reason to break up with him on the spot. Just keep those things in mind when you're figuring out if you want to be with him long term.

SINGING THE BEACH TOWN BLUES

After dating Chad for a few months, we decided to take a vacation together. He always preferred to drive because he didn't trust other drivers, yet he drove like my grandfather. He was cautious but drove way too slowly for my liking. At least he picked enjoyable music for me to sing along to on the way to the airport.

We were going to a beach town for a week, and I told him to pack mostly casual outfits, some clothes for hiking, a bathing suit, and one dress shirt and pants for a fancy evening out. I packed lightly and had a small carry-on suitcase that I pulled out of the backseat after he parked. I heard him grunting and looked in the trunk to find two gigantic suitcases that he was struggling to pull out of his car. I joked that he was smuggling a family of four to the beach before helping him slide the bags out.

We checked our luggage, went through security, and then walked to the food court before our flight. I already knew Chad suffered from anxiety, but he never told me how stressed out he gets on flights. While eating, he rummaged through his bag and pulled out a bottle of Xanax. He warned me that he was about to take a high dose of Xanax and would be drowsy soon. He wanted to be unconscious for the whole flight, and if he fell asleep before we got on the plane, he said I should shake him until he woke up and drag him to his seat.

I did not want to be forced to drag a drowsy, dizzy, unbalanced man onto a flight. Of course, as soon as we sat down at the gate, we were told that the flight was delayed, so I spent the next hour shaking him awake every minute to ensure he didn't fall asleep until we were seated on the plane.

Chad was mainly in a deep sleep during our six-hour flight. He rested his head on my shoulder and drooled for about four hours, and then for the other two hours, he gasped, woke up abruptly, and mumbled something incomprehensible before falling back to sleep.

I did have to shake Chad awake and drag him off of the plane when we landed, and I made him drink multiple cups of coffee from the food court to keep him awake for a little longer. I just had to accept that he wouldn't be back to his normal self until the Xanax wore off. Since he was pretty out of it, I had to roll his huge suitcases, in addition to mine, while dragging him to the cab. We made it to the hotel, and he promptly passed out for the night.

The next day, I jumped out of bed, eager to begin our vacation. I wanted to check out the beach, so I told him to put his bathing suit on so we could enjoy the ocean. He opened a suitcase, and I watched him pull out thirty identical white undershirts. I asked him why he brought so many, and he said he had backups in case he got overly sweaty. Understandable, I suppose, but that still seemed like overkill to me. Then I stared at him as he pulled out thirty similar tropical shirts. I had never seen him wear any of those before, and then he told me he bought them just for this vacation.

Since the first suitcase was mostly empty after taking out all those shirts, I was hoping the next suitcase would hold all the useful clothes. To my dismay, he pulled out twenty pairs of jeans and a boatload of sunscreen bottles, aloe vera, insect repellent, and other lotions. He forgot to pack a bathing suit, shorts, hiking clothes, and a dressy outfit—all the stuff I had specifically asked him to bring!

He agreed to buy a cheap bathing suit, but he didn't want to spend money on new sneakers or nice clothes. He said he'd be able to hike in his jeans and casual shoes. I had doubts, but I didn't argue. I already felt defeated, and our trip had just begun.

We got to the beach, and as we were walking in the sand to find a place to put down our stuff, this is the moment Chad decided to share that he was scared of the ocean. Despite living a few miles from the beach his whole life, he had never set foot in any ocean. I couldn't believe it! I had to hold his hand and slowly walk with him into the ocean. It would've been amusing if a shark brushed by his legs, but the water was clear and calm.

Our next misadventure was going on a hike. I had stretchy and breathable workout clothes on, while he had old, unsupportive shoes and thick, rigid jeans. Unsurprisingly, the hike didn't last long. Chad got overheated and complained of his feet aching.

We went back to the hotel, and I claimed the first shower. When I came out, I noticed that he had "organized" by spreading out his piles of identical clothes and lotions all over every free space in the room. He had taken over the entire room with his stuff and left a tiny corner for my suitcase. I shook my head in disbelief and started to realize that Chad was not the guy for me.

Chad could tell I was getting frustrated by some of the events from the past 24 hours, so he told me to put on my fancy outfit so he could take me somewhere special. I wore a cute dress, and he put on his jeans and tropical shirt. Everything was within walking distance from the hotel, so we walked a few blocks until he stopped in front of a beautiful building. He proudly pointed to the name of the restaurant, and I remembered hearing people rave about it earlier that day. He said he made a reservation, and he seemed thrilled to usher me in.

The hostess looked us both up and down and then said, "I'm sorry, but this is an upscale restaurant. No jeans allowed." Chad sulked, but I wasn't going to allow this teenager to kick us out. I pleaded with her and said he lost his luggage with his nice clothes. I begged her to make an exception. She wouldn't budge. She said she'd call security if we didn't leave at once.

The second we left the restaurant, a rain cloud opened up right above us and drenched us before we had a chance to escape. The timing was impeccable. I felt like we were in a cheesy movie, but I didn't see any happy ending for us at that point. As we were already soaked, we silently walked back to our hotel, with our heads hanging low. We dried off and changed and then ordered room service. The rest of our vacation was on par with the first day. I tried to laugh off all the problems we faced, but Chad wasn't in the laughing mood for the next six days.

My takeaway: This vacation taught me what Chad was like when he was out of his element. I wasn't planning on testing his behavior, but I discovered things about him that I wouldn't have known if we took a day trip somewhere. Experiencing the plane ride, seeing his packing skills, and being around someone with so much negativity opened my eyes to Chad's nature. He wasn't the type of guy I wanted to spend a lifetime with, and so this vacation brought it all to light.

Summary

The way a guy treats your waiter at a restaurant is indicative of how he'll treat you. Pay attention to his behavior when he's angry, drunk, facing an emergency, and going on vacation. You can assess his personality and decide if he's someone you want to continue dating.

CHAPTER 20
COULD'VE, WOULD'VE, SHOULD'VE

If you think back on all the dating mistakes you've made throughout your life, you'll go crazy. Don't beat yourself up for staying with the wrong guy for months or even years too long. It's all in the past, and you can learn from your mistakes and move on to find your perfect partner.

I *could've* been married three times by now if I had settled for a guy who was only mildly compatible with me. I *would've* said yes if any of them proposed, but I'm thankful that it never got that far. I *should've* broken up with these guys months before I did, but instead, I wasted years of my life in unhealthy relationships.

Don't dwell on the past. What's done is done. From reading my personal stories, you've probably noticed that I've had a variety of dating experiences. Most of the good ones aren't mentioned, but many bad ones are. I've shared these stories to remind you that everyone has a rocky past when it comes to love. Once you climb out of the rubble, you can brush off the dirt and learn from your dating mistakes.

SEX MISHAPS ARE ALWAYS FUNNY

I was dating a guy named Nick, who regularly complained about stomach pain. He was adventurous in bed and wanted to have sex all the time, despite his stomach issues. His sexual appetite was appealing to me, so I ignored his complaints and jumped into bed with him whenever we had the chance. After dating him for a while, I began to notice when his stomach hurt more than usual. He tried to hide his pain, but I could see the tension in his whole body.

One night, Nick came over, and I noticed the tension right away. He fought through his pain, gave me a seductive look, and ripped off his clothes. Rather than saying no, I ripped off my clothes and jumped into bed with him. We rolled around and tested out different positions, and then I ended up on top.

He opened his mouth to speak, and for a moment, I thought he was about to tell me he loved me for the first time. Instead, I saw a look of horror flash over his face. I asked what was wrong, and Nick said, "Don't worry about it. Just keep going." So I did. We kept moving back and forth, but I knew something was seriously wrong.

We finished having sex, and I rolled off of him and stood up. He usually got up to remove the condom, but this time he didn't move from the bed. I stared at him, and then he tried to shoo me out. He told me to go into the living room. I was confused, concerned, and intrigued. Why wasn't he getting up?

I refused to leave until he told me what was going on. He finally said, "I shit on the bed." I burst out laughing, because what else is there to do when a grown man says he took a shit on your favorite sheets? I urged him to get up and show me, and he did indeed shit on my bed. My laughter hid his embarrassment, and I continued using those sheets for the next ten years (after thoroughly washing them numerous times).

My takeaway: I *should've* said no to his sexual advances, but I didn't think about the consequences. I *would've* rejected him if I knew he couldn't control his bowels! After that night,

I learned that if my date has physical pain, especially in the stomach region, I will not engage in sexual activity of any kind.

HAPPILY NEVER AFTER

I went on a magical first date with James. He picked me up, took me to a popular restaurant, and walked along the beach with me as the stars glistened in the clear night sky. We bonded, laughed, and ended the date with a sweet kiss goodbye. When I got back to my apartment, I saw that James had just left me a voicemail message. I had a huge smile on my face as I put the phone up to my ear.

It began with him gushing about our superb night. He complimented me multiple times and said he couldn't wait to see me again. Then, he instantly stopped talking mid-sentence. I heard a crash, a pop, and a big groan from James, as if someone had just knocked the wind out of him. The smile disappeared from my face, and I pressed the phone closer to listen more intently. I heard movement, and then another voice said, "Can you get out? I just called 911." Then the message ended.

I left my apartment and ran down the hallway to my parking garage. I knew James couldn't have gone far, so I drove down the street and saw the accident within a few blocks. There were four cars that somehow all crashed into each other. I parked on the side of the road and went up to James. He was standing next to his car, looking dazed. He luckily didn't seem injured, but his car was totaled, and he could've had internal bleeding. I glanced over and noticed that the airbag had been deployed, which was the popping sound I heard. He was taken to the hospital in an ambulance, and I followed in my car.

James got a complete check-up at the hospital, and doctors didn't find anything wrong with him. I stayed with him all night to keep him company, and I drove him home to ensure he got back safely. Because the accident wasn't his fault, he received a hefty payout from the insurance companies that got him a brand new car.

We continued dating for a few months, but our dates were never as terrific as the first (pre-accident). I kept thinking he needed time to process his traumatic event, but things just felt off between us. We were having a deep discussion one day when I realized what the problem was. James blamed me for his car accident.

He said that if we hadn't gone out that night, or if he hadn't picked me up, or if we hadn't gone for a walk after dinner, or if he hadn't called me on his way home, the accident wouldn't have happened. I tried to explain that all those decisions were his (he asked me out, he offered to pick me up, he suggested taking a walk, and he called me while driving).

James wouldn't accept responsibility. He said he *could've* had a relaxing evening at home, and then he *would've* been able to keep his precious twenty-year-old Toyota Corolla. He also said he *should've* just stayed in Rhode Island, his home state, instead of moving across the country to Los Angeles.

He held a grudge from our first date, and that didn't go away. We never saw each other again, and I heard that he did move back home a few months later.

My takeaway: James made himself crazy with all the "could've, would've, should've" scenarios. He continued to blame others for his own actions and refused to take any responsibility. He wasn't injured and got a brand new car out of the accident, so he legitimately *should've* thanked me instead of treating me so badly.

SUMMARY

Don't dwell on the past. If you focus on what you could've, would've, and should've done, you'll miss out on your incredible future. You create your own destiny, so consider all your dating failures as learning experiences.

CLOSING REMARKS

After reading this book, you should now have the confidence to meet the man of your dreams. I wrote this book to send you on a clear path to love and romance. It's a cruel, harsh world, but love is what keeps us all going.

Instead of wasting your time on all the losers, idiots, and weirdos out there, you should now be better at picking out the sensational guys among the bunch.

FOLLOWING MY LESSONS WORKS!

If you're still skeptical that my dating techniques will help you find love, I'm the prime example of someone who made twenty-five years of dating mistakes until I followed my own advice. I knew what all the important lessons are when it comes to dating and relationships, but I often pushed my knowledge aside and made exceptions for guys more times than I care to admit.

Once I began writing my book and explaining why each and every lesson is vital to finding love, a clear picture started forming in my mind of *my* perfect man. I had recently broken up with a guy, and after completing the stages of grief (Chapter 1), I felt ready to get back into the dating world.

I'm no amateur at online dating (Chapter 2). Whenever I'm single, I have at least three dating apps on my phone that I consistently look through. This time around, I decided to join multiple Facebook singles groups as well. Instead of just focusing on my region, I joined worldwide groups.

Immediately after joining one of the Facebook groups, a profile caught my eye. The description of the guy was exactly what I was looking for, but there were no pictures. I noticed that all the comments stated that he's probably hideously ugly, but I didn't want to assume anything without learning more (Chapter 3).

I sent him a message with a short bio of myself, and he sent me some pictures, which were thankfully fantastic. We talked that night, and I felt instant phone chemistry in our first conversation. We unfortunately lived 1,000 miles apart, but we didn't let that stop us from having phone and video chats every few days.

We decided to drive and meet in the middle after two months of deep discussions. This was during a pandemic, so we felt that driving was the safest option for us. We arrived, and I made sure to follow all my dating rules before, during, and after our time together (Chapter 4).

I discovered possible red flags (Chapter 5), so I openly communicated my concerns with him. After hearing his responses, I began to like him even more. I could tell he was a trustworthy guy with excellent values.

There was no doubt in my mind that he was straight (Chapter 6) and that we were in the same stage of life (Chapter 7). I didn't want to rush our relationship status after knowing him for such a short time (Chapter 8), but I was confident that our relationship was proceeding nicely.

After all our long talks in person and on the phone, I felt that we had complete compatibility (Chapter 9). We were both single (Chapter 10), and he willingly got tested for STDs following an honest discussion about sex (Chapter 11). I felt like I was the truest version of myself I had ever been (Chapter 12), and he seemed to love and appreciate the real me.

We were both mentally healthy and had no addictions (Chapter 13), so I was thrilled for our potential future. My five senses were buzzing with electricity whenever I thought about him (Chapter 14), and my intuition told me that this was the real deal (Chapter 15).

I didn't want to make the mistake of my past where I spontaneously moved to a new city for a guy I barely knew (Chapter 16), so we stayed in regular contact virtually and agreed to meet in person as many times as we needed until we were sure we wanted to be together forever.

I'm the most impatient person in the world, so I *hate* waiting for a guy in any way (Chapter 17). Luckily, he wanted our relationship to progress just as quickly as I did, and he made every effort to move things along.

We spent hours discussing our requirements and needs in a relationship, and we determined that we wanted the exact same things (Chapter 18).

Our first time meeting in person was the ultimate vacation test (Chapter 19), and he passed with flying colors. Any fears or worries I had about my past melted away (Chapter 20), and all I saw was a bright future with him.

After twenty-five years of dating hundreds of losers and making awful mistakes in love, I believed in myself and my ability to attract exactly what I wanted in a partner. It hasn't been a simple road to love, but I finally found what I've been searching for my whole life—I finally found my soulmate! I put in work, effort, and self-discovery to attract the man of my dreams.

You can do it, too.

WHAT'S NEXT:
YOUR ROAD TO ROMANCE

Are you frustrated with singles events, online dating, being set up, and watching everyone around you get married while you remain single?

It's time to stop feeling sorry for yourself and take ownership of your love life!

With my 8-week coaching program, you will feel empowered and learn the skills you need to find your ideal mate.

We'll figure out your limiting beliefs and help you eliminate them. I'll take you through various exercises so you can visualize your perfect partner. I'll help you discover what your values and relationship requirements are.

Once you're ready to attract the right guy, we'll discuss how you can improve your dating and intimacy skills. I'll teach you how to expand your social network and develop proper techniques to attract your soulmate.

Coaching is a collaborative process. We'll focus on what you can do differently to resolve your dating dilemmas and find the man of your dreams.

My goal is for you to find love and be in a happy, healthy relationship. When I assist you with that process, I will be thrilled to make your dreams come true. As long as you commit to doing the work, you will find what you are looking for.

www.LoveLaughLeisure.com

ACKNOWLEDGMENTS

I would like to thank my mom for putting the idea of writing a book into my head. What a waste it would be to have all these adventures and not share them with anyone.

Thank you to Patti Britton, who not only wrote the foreword for my book, but also guided me onto the coaching path. I am forever grateful for this gift.

Thank you to every man I've been on a date with. Without those experiences, I wouldn't have a story to tell or dating lessons to pass on.

A big thank you goes out to my book coach, Ben Gioia, for motivating me to complete this book with efficiency and "heart" (following his "influence with a heart" method). I would also like to thank Chris O'Byrne, my publisher from Jetlaunch, who helped make this dream a reality.

Thanks to David Gannon and Robert Goodman for editing my book and confirming that my stories are all relatable and my lessons are universally applicable.

REFERENCES

The Art of Sex Coaching: Expanding Your Practice by Patti Britton

In Sickness and in Mental Health: Living with and Loving Someone with Mental Illness by Diane Mintz

Major Histocompatibility Complex: Evolution, Structure, and Function by Masanori Kasahara

On Death and Dying by Elisabeth Kubler-Ross

The Seasons of a Man's Life by Daniel Levinson

ABOUT THE AUTHOR

Rachel Scheer is a Certified Relationship Coach who helps savvy women find their perfect partners without the usual heartache. She has given relationship talks to thousands of people across the globe.

Rachel grew up in Cincinnati, Ohio and has lived all over the country. She currently resides in Sarasota, Florida, where she is often found at the beach watching the spectacular sunset.

In addition to coaching, Rachel enjoys singing, performing in theatrical productions, playing board games, and staying fit and healthy.